Don't Be a Stranger
Russian Literature and the
Perils of Not Fitting In

Don't Be a Stranger

Russian Literature and the Perils of Not Fitting In

Jason Galie

BOSTON
2022

This book was prepared by the author in his personal capacity. The views and opinions expressed in this book are those of the author and do not necessarily reflect the official policy, opinion, or position of their employer.

Library of Congress Cataloging-in-Publication Data: the bibliographic data for this title is available from the Library of Congress.

Copyright © Academic Studies Press, 2022

ISBN 9798887190952 (pbk.)
ISBN 9781644697733 (adobe pdf)
ISBN 9781644697740 (epub)
Book design by Lapiz Digital Services
Cover design by Ivan Grave

Published by Academic Studies Press
1577 Beacon Street
Brookline, MA 02446, USA
press@academicstudiespress.com
www.academicstudiespress.com

To my parents, Francis and Mary Galie

Contents

Acknowledgements	xi
Note on Transliteration	xiii
Introduction: Fitting in Russian Style	1
1. The Crux of the Svoj/Chuzhoj Opposition	13
2. Making Svoj/Chuzhoj Divisive in Aleksandr Griboedov's "Woe from Wit"	33
3. "Woe from Wit" as Social Gospel	69
4. The Demons are Social	91
Demons	100
The Setting	100
The Plot	103
The Audience and the Stage	104
The Opposition	106
Verkhovensky	106
A Stranger's Sins	108
The First Argument	111
The Second Argument	112
The Duel	113
At Our People's	115
The Murder of Shatov	118
In Place of a Conclusion	131
Bibliography	139
Primary Sources	139
Secondary Sources	140
Index	145

В такую погоду свои дома сидят, телевизор смотрят. Только чужие шастают. Не будем дверь открывать!
—"Трое из Простоквашино"

(People in our clan [*svoi*] sit at home in weather like this, watching television. Only outsiders [*chuzhie*] are roaming around. We are not opening the door!"
—From "Three from Prostokvashino")

Acknowledgements

It is an irony of this project that the study and teaching abroad opportunities that allowed me to comprehend Russia and Russian culture on a more substantial level are also what led me to believe that there is something within the culture that makes it resistant and even suspicious of these very cultural exchanges; at the very least, I came to believe that Russians have diminished expectations of what they can accomplish.

In any case, it was on one of these cultural exchanges that I began to notice, as I eventually found a group of Russian friends, how often I was encountering the rhymed words *svoj* and *chuzhoj*, specifically as they referred to people. At first, I heard them in speech, but later I began to see them in print as well, in newspapers, books, and advertisements. As I began to grasp on the most general level what concepts lay behind these terms, I realized that the English translations of them fell woefully short. Each time I encountered them, I found myself translating them in my mind using a different English word. The words *svoj* and *chuzhoj* are used across far too many registers and in far too many genres to be translated with the same two discrete English terms.

As I grew closer to this group of Russians, I was able to experience first-hand what it feels like to be accepted as *svoj chelovek* (*one of us*). The feelings of safety and camaraderie inherent in this relationship are powerful. So powerful, in fact, that one would be forgiven in thinking that there is no downside to the relationship at all.

The first time I was able to apply my thoughts on this opposition in an academic setting was as a graduate student in the early 2000s in Irina Reyfman's Early Russian Drama course at Columbia University. A class presentation on Aleksandr Griboedov's play *Woe from Wit* led to further fruitful discussion with Irina, who eventually became my dissertation advisor. This book is an expansion of that 2007 dissertation, entitled *The Clan, the Clique, and the Alien in Russian Literature and Society*. I of course owe Irina a great deal of gratitude for her contributions to both the dissertation and this project in general. Ron Meyer at the Harriman Institute provided invaluable feedback on the manuscript, as did Valeria Sobol and Rich Robin. I thank them all.

I must also thank my first Russian friends in St. Petersburg who accepted a naïve American as one of their own. But my deepest gratitude goes out to the White Nights and to each and every St. Petersburg bridge that remained open for hours in the summer of 1999. Thanks to them, I was forced to spend many a night with these friends on the Petrogradskaya storona where I eventually became *svoj*.

Note on Transliteration

I have followed the Library of Congress guidelines on transliteration with exceptions made for the words *свой, чужой,* and *изгой.* Here I use the letter "j" for Cyrillic "й," to differentiate the singular *свoj* from the plural *свои.*

Introduction: Fitting in Russian Style

It is now commonplace to remark on how interconnected the world has become; that we are all "citizens of the world," to quote Martha Nussbaum who paraphrases Diogenes in her book *Cultivating Humanity: A Classical Defense of Reform in Liberal Education*. College curricula in North America and Europe are being revamped constantly to emphasize multiculturalism and diversity, all in an attempt to give equal space to disparate customs, values, and experiences. The study of foreign languages and cultures is viewed as essential to an effective understanding of this diversity and its place in the world in which college graduates will operate. But what happens if, during the course of studying a foreign language and culture, one that you should presumably respect, you discover a linguistic and cultural opposition so powerful that it seems to impose a world view on its speakers that rejects the incorporation of others' customs, lifestyles, and viewpoints? One that drives a palpable wedge between one's own people and the rest of society?

Many writers have commented on the startling contrast between the often brusque, dismissive behavior that Russians display towards strangers on the street and the warmth and generosity they show at home, behind closed doors. These doors, often imposing, metallic structures accessible only with an equally formidable, weapon-like key, separate the public and the private, and, perhaps more importantly, the stranger or the alien, from one's own people or one's own clan. Once this sanctum has been breached, however, a heady mixture of argument, cigarette smoke, and delectable food awaits. However, not everyone can be admitted. Not everyone can be trusted. After you ring the ear-splitting buzzer next to a typical Russian apartment door, the password that will grant you entry after the barked "*Kto??*" (Who??) from the other side is not your name or the name of the person you are hoping to see. No, the magic word is the much more nebulous "*Svoi.*"[1] This word, *svoi*, or more specifically its singular form, *svoj*, is difficult to translate, but its meaning can be rendered as "one of us/one of the group/one of the clan." When someone has been dubbed "*svoj*," or "*svoj chelovek*" (a person who is one of us) in Russian society, the group that has bestowed the status is confirming, in effect, that that person has always been there, that her presence is a given, and, perhaps most importantly, that everyone around her can let their guard down.[2] The person in question is easy to talk to and will be capable of understanding everyone else in the group immediately. She *knows* and is *known*. All pretenses are dropped. Although the designation has little to do with age, gender, or socio-economic status, it doesn't mean there are no criteria at all for membership.

There is an opposite pole, however, to the word *svoj*— its rhymed counterpart, "*chuzhoj*" (stranger, alien, outsider, foreigner), a label, as we shall see, to be avoided at all costs in present-day Russian society.

"So what?"—one might say. Doesn't everyone pick and choose the individuals they want to associate with, excluding significantly more people than they include? In a word, yes. The desire to fit in is certainly not specific to Russian culture. David Berreby makes this very point in *Us and Them: Understanding Your Tribal Mind*: "There is apparently no people known to history or anthropology that lacks a distinction between 'us' and 'others.' Dividing people into overlapping categories is something all human beings do (with exceptions for which there are ready explanations, usually involving brain damage)" (125).

Olga Yokoyama, in her article *Russian Genderlects and Referential Expressions*, also points out that other cultures express the distinction between "one's own" and "others/aliens/strangers." She sees something unique, however, in the manner in which Russians categorize people along these lines: "There is no

---

1 The response is in the plural even if the person attempting to access the apartment is alone, effectively capturing the notion that it is more important that a group of such people exists than that an individual member is at the door, awaiting entry.
2 This project involves an analysis of the opposition in Russian culture, literature, and society. Although my research was somewhat superficial, it seems the two words, in their respective variants, interact in a similar fashion in Ukrainian and Belarusian. It would be an interesting project to delve deeper into the opposition in the other two East Slavic worlds.

doubt, though, that the English also have their own way to make distinctions between their relatives and others/strangers/aliens. The radius for what they consider their own people, however, cannot compare in scope with a Russian's" (401–429). One of the differences particular to the Russian context does indeed lie in this scope, to be sure, but there is more to the story. Another difference is twofold and can be found both in the criteria used to bestow or deny the status of *svoj* and in the consequences that result from the decision (especially if an individual or group is deemed unworthy). In other words, there is much more at stake for a Russian speaker than there is for someone from another culture when that individual is confronted by (his culture's version of) the opposition.

Take the fundamental human activity of oral communication, for instance. Yokoyama argues that native speakers of Russian base their very *conversational strategies* on the extent to which their interlocutor is perceived as *svoj*: "One might extend this to suggest that, in Japanese, speakers' awareness of their sex is fundamental to their cognitive/linguistic universe; but in Russian, the primary task of the speaker is to determine the degree of "svoj-ness," i.e. the degree of distance between the self and the addressee" (417). If the degree of "svoj-ness" is high, the interlocutor presumably gains access to an altogether different (more intimate) manner of interaction, a manner that encompasses both form and content.

Perhaps because of the perceived high stakes involved in the matter, one sociologist with whom I have corresponded claims that a Russian's entire existence can be reduced to a lifelong search for his own people (*svoi*). Anna Shor-Chudnovskaya, a sociologist and researcher at the Sigmund Freud University, Vienna, states:

> Русский человек мучительно ищет Своих. Если Вы посмотрите диссидентскую литературу 20-го века, там будет все время повторяться эта тема— как выйти к Своим. И на фоне этого мучительно поиска, русского человека совершенно не интересует, как нужно, положено (нравственно) обращаться с Чужими (уважать их права и т.п.). Отношения с Чужими— это формальные (рыночные) отношения буржуазного мира. Отношения со Своими—это родственные, дружеские, как и говорят по-русски, свойские отношения. И именно потому, как мне представляется, что в российском обществе очень слабо выражены формальные отношения, так важно и так тяжело понять, кто Свой, а кто Чужой— понять-то это хочется окончательно! Русский человек верит в

"окончательно Своих", "Своих навсегда",—"Своих, заданных Свыше"? (Personal communication)

A Russian is on an excruciating search for One's Own People. If you look at the dissident literature of the twentieth century, this theme repeats itself over and over—how to reach One's Own People. And in the context of this excruciating search, a Russian is completely uninterested in how he is expected (morally) to treat Strangers/Aliens (respecting their rights, etc). Contact with Strangers/Aliens constitutes formal (market) relations of the bourgeois world. Contact with One's Own is a kindred, friendly, as they say in Russian, chummy kind of relationship. And, to my mind, for the very reason that formal contact is so weakly defined in Russian society, it becomes so crucial and difficult to figure out just who is One of Us and who is a Stranger/Alien. And people want to figure it out once and for all! A Russian is certain of "a conclusive group of one's own," "a group of one's own forever"—"a group of one's own destined from Above"?

My intention in this book, then, is to show that modern-day Russians require a certain set of almost unobtainable criteria from those with whom they interact in order for them to find those people trustworthy. My project incorporates an analysis of a specific worldview and how that worldview has been shaped by the way in which Russians use and interpret the two aforementioned words, *svoj* and *chuzhoj*. The book will illuminate, for the Western reader especially, how the opposition presents an at times insurmountable hurdle before a native Russian speaker on the path to the kind of world citizenship (or even Russian citizenship) advocated by Martha Nussbaum. I should point out, to my Western readers especially, that Russian speakers are exposed to this opposition from the moment they begin to process their parents' voices and begin to learn the language. Its negative pole, *chuzhoj*, then, cannot serve as a translation of the (Western) concept of "the Other."[3] "The Other" is a cultural construct not necessarily reflected in the language and lacking a related lexical pair; the words *svoj* and *chuzhoj*, on the other hand, interact closely with each other to this day in every linguistic register. If Russian academics had indeed decided to translate

---

3 The word in Russian is usually rendered as the formerly archaic, now relatively neutral, Иной (*Inoi*).

"the Other" as *Chuzhoj*, someone would most likely have immediately posed the question, "Well, then, what/who is *Svoj*?"

The project will prove useful to Russian speakers as well, as it is my belief that although native Russians are quite aware of the opposition and its use, they are perhaps too closely aligned with it to consider it worthy of deep exploration. That is to say, they are aware of it in a way that precludes an unbiased assessment. That said, lengthy articles have been published by Russian-speaking writers using the opposition as a lens to interpret many works of literature and concepts in Russian culture;[4] This scholarly output, however, stops short of questioning the lens itself or how it came into existence. Since the two components of the binary are not *completely* untranslatable, especially into other Slavic languages, many Russians would, and do, state that these concepts are not unique to their language and culture. That argument is not without merit. However, my aim is to show that Russians perceive, evaluate, and subsequently treat those who have been dubbed *svoj* or *chuzhoj* in demonstrably different ways than Americans or French people do when categorizing people into the groups that most closely correspond to those terms in English or French.

This treatment (of those dubbed *chuzhoj*, specifically) led Christof Ruhl of the World Bank to remark, in 2004, on Russians and their society: "The people just don't care. On a very broad scale, it's a country where people care about their family and friends. Their clan. But not their society." Elaborating on that sentiment, Nancy Ries, in her book, *Russian Talk*, a socio-anthropological investigation into the Russian manner of conversing during the time of Perestroika, describes the shunned *chuzhie* (the plural form of *chuzhoj*) as evil in Russians' minds, pointing to their "... conviction that there is an unbridgeable chasm between good selves and evil others, or in Russian vernacular, 'ours' and 'alien' (*svoj-chuzhoj*)" (114).

This perceived "unbridgeable chasm" has shaped contemporary Russian society in significant ways and contributed to a certain level of dysfunctionality. If you trust only a small group of people in your life, it is difficult to imagine large protest movements (or even neighborhood watch groups) operating effectively. Ries, again: "This kind of ideology effectively reduces the ability to perceive social groups as interdependent and may impede mediating processes at many levels of society, even the most immediate and local" (114).

---

4 These works and concepts include: Nikolai Chernyshevsky's *Chto delat'* (*What is to be Done?*), the works of Nadezhda Khvoshchinskaya and Boris Pasternak, and the troika versus the train in Russian culture. These articles are found in the 1995 collection *"Svoe" i "Chuzhoe" v literature i kul'ture* (One's own and the foreign in literature and culture).

There are, after all, practical advantages to cultivating relationships with those outside your close-knit circle of friends and family, a practice discussed at length in *The Strength of Weak Ties* (1973), a seminal article by Mark Granovetter, Professor of Sociology at Stanford University. Granovetter explores in-depth the importance of more distant relationships to an effective social network. Granovetter here describes the hypothetical job search of a member of a social group, but the sentiment can be applied to the viability of most any social structure: "[T]hose to whom we are weakly tied are more likely to move in circles different from our own and will thus have access to information different from that which we receive" (1371). He goes on to speak of the harm that can result in ignoring or not making full use of people outside of your close circle of friends and family. Now, if you will, imagine the consequences in the Russian context, where these people are often actively shunned.

But this tendency to avoid and denigrate perceived outsiders has not always been present in Russia; there are, I will argue, specific time periods and works of literature that set Russian society on a certain path and then accelerated its progress. This book traces that path in detail, beginning in the eighteenth century, a time when the words *svoj/chuzhoj* certainly existed as antonyms, but when the negative pole did not result in significant harm to those who had acquired the status. The word *svoj* was most often used in reference to one's family members and, at times, servants.

The memoirs of E. P. Yankova (1768–1861), eventually published by her grandson in 1885 under the title *Grandmother's Stories: Memories of Five Generations* (Rasskazy babushki: iz vospominanii pyati pokolenii) contain numerous examples of the opposition operating within a network of closely and not-so-closely related noblemen and women of the time. The stories depict the interaction of Yankova's relations via the system of *svoistvo*[5] (relationship by marriage), which of course contains the word *svoj*. The negative pole of the opposition was used to describe people with whom one did not have a close relationship. These people may have even been "friends," in the looser definition of the word we have seen in circulation since the appearance of Facebook (in Russian, people one friended on Facebook—*frendy*—are decidedly not the same as *druz'ya—friends*).

Moving ahead to the early part of the nineteenth century and Aleksandr Griboedov's beloved drama *Woe from Wit* (*Gore ot uma*), I demonstrate that the work marks a crucial and devastating shift in the interpretation of the word *chuzhoj*. The shift occurs during the ball scene when Sofya Famusova dubs her

---

5 With the accent on the final syllable.

childhood friend Aleksandr Chatsky "insane," doing so by using very specific wording ("не в своем уме"— "not in his [right] mind"). This "diagnosis" results in Chatsky's eventual departure from a group of people he thought was "his own" (*svoi*). It is not just the content of *Woe from Wit* that impacted the opposition, however. The manner in which the work was received and disseminated (for decades) in Russian society also affected the ways in which the opposition operated. The play and its reception fundamentally changed the criteria that Russians now use to accept people into their inner circles (*svoi*) as well as marking the moment when the social interpretation of the words began to dominate.

My last chapter travels even further into the nineteenth century, to the 1870s specifically, to Fyodor Dostoevsky's *Demons* (*Besy*). On a fundamental level, I consider this novel to be the author's attempt to correct Russian society's insistence on using a rigid and entirely social interpretation of the *svoj/chuzhoj* opposition when evaluating a person. I will show that Dostoevsky was very well acquainted with Griboedov's play and with the effect it had had on the Russian reader earlier in the century. In *Demons*, the author uses the reader's familiarity with *Woe from Wit* to accomplish a certain goal, namely, to try to steer the reader away from a purely social interpretation of the opposition.

By the time *Demons* was published, the word *chuzhoj* had acquired extremely negative connotations as well as the ability to inflict real damage. This damage is clearly laid out in the opening pages of Tolstoy's *Anna Karenina*, also written in the 1870s. After Dolly Oblonsky discovers her husband Stiva's infidelity, she makes a quick inventory of the words at her disposal to express her anger— even uttering a few conventional ones—but she ultimately decides that the word *chuzhoj* would serve as the most effective insult. Tolstoy even has the narrator step in to emphasize the difficulty Dolly has in uttering the epithet: "'Вы мне мерзки, гадки, чужой, да, чужой совсем!—с болью и злобой произнесла она это ужасное для себя слово *чужой*" ("'You are vile, loathsome, a stranger, yes, a stranger!'—and painfully, spitefully, the terrible word 'stranger' fell from her lips,'" part 1, section 4). The English translation of the word, especially in this context, is decidedly inadequate, even comical—is "stranger" more terrible than "loathsome" or "vile"? To a Russian, however, her sentiments made perfect sense (and still do). In *Demons*, Dostoevsky endeavors to show the harm that can result from granting this word so much power. To drive this point home throughout the novel, Dostoevsky uses various methods to illuminate for the reader what he considers to be alternate and entirely valid interpretations of the opposition, interpretations that Russians have somehow managed to forget.

This project's theoretical framework, especially on the topic of "forgotten" meanings of the word *chuzhoj*, relies on the work of the Soviet semioticians. I refer in particular to an article by V. V. Ivanov and V. N. Toporov from 1965 entitled "Slavic linguistic modeling semiotic systems" ("Slavyanskie yazykovye modeliruyushchie sistemy"). Most subsequent scholarly treatments of the opposition reference this article as the first to address the subject. Here the authors separate the spheres in which the opposition manifests itself into the social, ethnic, and supernatural. According to the authors, the social interpretation includes groups of people that are to some extent interconnected; the *chuzhoj* member would be anyone that cannot be viewed as a primary symbol (*preimushchestvennyi simvol*) of the given (*svoj*) group. The ethnic interpretation, in turn, is concerned with the ancient enemies (*chuzhie*) of the Slavs (*svoi*), and includes the Tatar and the nomad, or, in mythological manifestations, the Russian folk characters Zmei-Tugarin, Idolishche, and Solov ei-razboinik. The supernatural deals with the divide between the human (*svoj*) and the inhuman, beastly, or magical worlds (all *chuzhoj*).

The semioticians point out, however, that a certain fluidity exists among the categories; in many cases a person or entity could be perceived as both (or either) *svoj* and/or *chuzhoj*. For example, Ivanov and Toporov begin with a discussion of the pagan gods of the East Slavic and Iranian worlds. Although the authors divide the deities into East Slavic *svoi bogi* (one's own gods) and Iranian *chuzhie bogi* (foreign/outsider gods), they recognize a blending of the two from a very early stage. This blending can be seen in the assimilation of a number of Iranian gods into the East Slavic pantheon. The authors assert that this phenomenon occurs in both the ethnic and social spheres as well.

In the realm of fairy tales, mythology, and the supernatural, the Slavic characters Baba-Yaga (the witch), Rusalka (the mermaid), and Medved' (the bear) appear occasionally as *svoj* and occasionally as *chuzhoj*. In fact, Vladimir Propp, in his 1946 *Historical Roots of the Fairy Tale* (*Istoricheskie korni volshebnoi skazki*), defines three types of Baba-Yaga:

> At a basic level, the fairy tale contains three different forms of Yaga. For example, there is the Gift-Giver Yaga, whom the hero visits. She quizzes him and he (or the heroine) receives a steed, expensive gifts, etc. Another type is the Child-Snatcher Yaga. She kidnaps children and attempts to fry them up, after which an escape and rescue ensue. Finally, there is the Warrior Yaga. She flies into the heroes' huts, flays them and makes a belt out of the skin and so forth. (53)

Baba-Yaga, along with many other East Slavic mythological characters, also possesses the ability to change her shape (she is an *oboroten'*, or changeling).

Ivanov and Toporov point to the Rusalka as a prime example of the fluidity that exists between the designations *svoj* and *chuzhoj*: "In principle it is possible to cross over from the foreign/strange/alien/supernatural to one's own/human and vice versa; an example of the first instance would be the baptism of mermaids after which it is possible to marry them; of the second instance, the transformation of a human who has died an unnatural death into an evil spirit" (159–160).

We can find further evidence of the fluidity that these scholars see between the *svoj/chuzhoj* designations in the Medved'. In Slavic cultures, the Medved' is also both *svoj* and *chuzhoj* in the sense that he belongs to the human world and to the non-human. Ivanov and Toporov provide a number of examples of the bear fulfilling both roles in East Slavic folklore. As the authors explain, the Medved', usually referred to as Misha, Mikhail Ivanovich, or Mikhailo Potapych, often performs a positive deed for the Russian people in fairy tales. Many ancient wedding rituals in both West and East Slavic cultures involve the invocation of the bear as a source of good luck and a happy marriage. The bear does not always portend good things, however. In many fairy tales he is portrayed as the lord of the forest, dangerous to humans and livestock alike. He eats people, kidnaps the tsar's children, and generally terrorizes the land.

Yuri Lotman and Boris Uspensky, in their 1982 article "'Izgoi' and 'izgoinichestvo' as socio-psychological position in Russian culture primarily of the pre-Petrine period" ("'Izgoi' i 'izgoinichestvo' kak sotsial' no-psikhologicheskaya pozitsiya v russkoi kul'ture preimyshchestvenno dopetrovskogo perioda"), in which they also explore the *svoj/chuzhoj* opposition, mention the bear, again as a kind of shape-changer: "It should be emphasized that an *izgoj* could be directly identified with a sorcerer-changeling. Thus, a renegade whose behavior contradicted the behavior of society as a whole could be called 'a bear'" (114).[6] According to the authors, these sorcerers and shamans were regarded as both *svoj* and *chuzhoj* in pre-Petrine Russia; they were feared but, at the same time,

---

6 An *izgoj* is defined thusly: "(From old Russian *goit'*, to live), persons in 11th- and 12th-century Rus' who were displaced by circumstances from their normal social position. The earliest references to these people are found in the Russkaia Pravda (earliest Russian law code), in the law code of Prince Rostislav Mstislavich of Smolensk (1150), and in the ecclesiastical statutes of Prince Vsevolod Gavriil Mstislavich. *Izgoi* lived on the lands of both lay and ecclesiastical feudal lords. Most of them appear to have been either peasants whose connection with the rural commune had been broken during feudalization or slaves who had bought or been granted their freedom. With the development of feudalism this group gradually became part of the feudally dependent population as a whole" (*The Great Soviet Encyclopedia*, https://encyclopedia2.thefreedictionary.com/Izgoi).

often highly respected. These figures were often extremely knowledgeable, perhaps the main character trait that inspired both the fear and the respect. Lotman and Uspensky claim that people in professions that required the learning of secrets and mysteries and the accumulation of knowledge in general were usually regarded as *chuzhie*. Roma often worked as farriers and blacksmiths and thus were considered suspicious. In post-Petrine Russia, foreigners were to be found in professions that required special knowledge, perhaps contributing to the strengthening of the ethnic sphere of the opposition. One example of this would be the German domination of the medical profession in Russia until well into the nineteenth century.

Acquiring the status of an *izgoj*, according to Lotman and Uspensky, requires some sort of expulsion from an authoritative organization or social group. This expulsion often results in the *izgoj* then wandering aimlessly, sleeping in all sorts of locations: "A person who is 'on the outside,' is excluded from social structures; spatially he lives *outside*—outside of home, roaming the streets and sleeping under fences (or in taverns, in modern times in railway stations, in whatever can *not* be considered lodging), wandering the roads, living in the forest or in graveyards or settling outside the city limits" (116). This depiction of an expelled renegade wandering the land will be crucial for my discussions of Ivan Shatov in *Demons*.

It happens that when *izgoi* find each other in their roamings, they may decide to form a community. One example of such a community would be the *razboiniki* (bandits), a group that has existed in Russia since the times of Rus' in direct opposition to organized government. But the lines between these rogues and the upstanding citizens of the land were not always so clearly drawn. The authors claim that in the sixteenth and seventeenth centuries, even landowners and innkeepers engaged in robbery on the high roads at night, leading a kind of double life. In any case, because these bandits pursued a lifestyle so at odds with the establishment, they took on certain mythological traits and were associated with werewolves and changelings.

A signature aspect of these bandits' behavior, and one that will also be vital to my discussion of Shatov, is their involvement in the search for and excavation of buried treasure. For Lotman and Uspensky, buried treasure is protected by evil spirits (*nechistaya sila*), which are equated with pagan gods, and any success in unearthing said treasure is linked with the ability to communicate with these forces. These bandits often signal each other by whistling: "The characteristic trait of a bandit is whistling (whistling being the traditional means by which one invokes evil spirits). The whistle is the distinguishing signal, a kind of bandit "uniform," by which he is recognized by others" (117). This whistle signal will also prove useful in my reading of *Demons*.

In his 1997 *Constants: Dictionary of Russian Culture* (*Konstanty: slovar' russkoi kul' tury*), Yuri Stepanov devotes an entire section to the opposition *svoj/ chuzhoj* and its implications for the supernatural as well as the ethnic and social. He begins this section with a general culturological introduction followed by a description of the origins and evolution of the opposition, its prehistory and etymology in Indo-European languages, and its manifestations in people's social interactions. The dictionary examines the opposition's relevance for the categories of ethnicity and magic. Stepanov looks at the similarities between the words *chuzhoj* and чудо (*chudo*—"miracle"). He points out that Russians have long perceived certain northern peoples— the Chud', for example (the name of the tribe suggests another possible origin for the word *chuzhoj*)— as sorcerers and magicians.

Much of the critical works that have appeared since Ivanov and Toporov's article treat the word *chuzhoj* and the people so designated as highly negative, almost, as Nancy Ries writes, as "evil." Looking at contemporary Russian culture and history through the lens of this opposition, it is difficult to disagree with such an interpretation. However, as the semioticians have pointed out, the label *chuzhoj* did not always carry with it such a stigma, certainly in the supernatural realm, but also in the social sphere. The *svoj* designation was considered, to be sure, a significant boon that brought with it many benefits to the person so dubbed. But there was a time when to be *chuzhoj* meant merely to be not *svoj*, not "one of us," without the later pejorative connotations that became attached to it.

These connotations are conveyed convincingly in the Russian translation of the title of the 1979 Ridley Scott film "Alien." The title was (effectively) rendered into Russian as *Chuzhoj* despite the fact that all English-Russian dictionaries of which I am aware list *inozemets* or *inostranets* (foreigner) as the first entries for the English word "alien." Neither of these words, however, captures the sense of foreboding and terror present on the movie posters alone. Yes, one might say, but the movie is about a *space* alien, not a foreigner, not a human being from another country. The translation for "space alien" in Russian, however, is *inoplanetyanin* (extraterrestrial), a word that conjures up the world of animation and green antenna in a Russian's mind, certainly not the genre the filmmakers were interested in. Without doubt, the most accurate (and terrifying) one-word translation of the film's title into Russian is *Chuzhoj*. This is the word that evokes the maximum amount of fear in the Russian viewer. This is the word that most accurately describes the monstrous entity that massacres the crew of a spaceship one by one and reproduces by implanting its eggs inside the bodies of humans. The egg later grows and hatches, exploding its host's rib cage from the inside.[7]

The danger posed by the *chuzhie* is also present in the ethnic realm. After the fall of the Soviet Union, in particular, many ethnic Russians (living in Russia) have been unsure how to categorize the residents of the former republics, although it is safe to say that the darker the person's skin, the more difficult the transition has been for citizens of the former Soviet Union. The current hot topic of legal and illegal migration is even more controversial in the Russian context; Tajik guest workers in Moscow are often not Russian citizens, but many of them were most certainly *Soviet* citizens before 1991. Are they completely *chuzhie*? And what about ethnic Russians born and raised in Latvia? Many speak only Russian but have never been to Russia even once. What are they? This project will shed light on why these questions are so urgent for contemporary Russians and will attempt to explain the events that have put Russia on what I would call a collision course with the "the West" when it comes to evaluating different cultures and peoples.

It is my hope that this book will prove useful not only to those interested in Russian literature but to students of contemporary Russian society and culture as well. It is my firm belief that anyone interested in Russia in any capacity must understand the importance that literature plays in all aspects of life there. My project intends to move beyond the dictate we often give students to read some Russian literature to understand the culture. There are reasons that Russians value literature, especially certain works of literature. There are reasons that close familiarity with the Russian canon helps you fit in. And there are reasons that fitting in is the ultimate goal.

---

7 A literal imagining of *chuzhoj sredi svoikh* (a stranger amidst one's own).

Chapter One

The Crux of the Svoj/Chuzhoj Opposition

For a non-native speaker of Russian wishing to make a serious attempt at understanding the language and culture, certain words and concepts become marked at a fairly early stage. I am speaking of words like *dusha* (soul), *sud' ba* (fate, destiny), *toska* (longing, sorrow), *porog* (threshold), *narod* (the people), and, most important for the present project, the enigmatic *svoj* and *chuzhoj*. This chapter offers a cultural and literary investigation into the words *svoj* and *chuzhoj* and into their interaction on Russian soil in roughly the first quarter of the nineteenth century.

Although the words *svoj* and *chuzhoj* exist in all Slavic languages in some form (stemming from the same Proto-Slavic roots), they interact as an opposition only in the three East Slavic languages— Ukrainian, Belorussian, and Russian. In all Slavic languages *svoj* means "one's own" when it refers to ownership, and *chuzhoj* means "someone else's" or "foreign." The definition of the words that most interests me, however, and that will be the subject of my discussion, is the one used to evaluate a *person*. This definition is always given a separate entry in a Russian dictionary. For example, the *Great Interpretive Dictionary of the Russian Language* (*Bol'shoi tolkovyi slovar' russkogo yazyka*), published in 1998, defines the word *chuzhoj* in the following manner:

1.) Belonging to another (others); lacking a direct relationship to someone; not one's own (*ne svoj*). 2.) Not of the motherland, not resembling what is to be found in the motherland. 3.) Not connected by blood relations; extraneous. 4.) Not connected by close relations with someone, not agreeing in spirit, outlook, interests; extraneous, distant. 5.) Estranged, aloof.

My project will chiefly address definitions two through five, although not exclusively.

The words *svoj* and *chuzhoj*, when referring to people, do not mean quite the same thing in their variants in other Slavic languages, and they do not interact as an opposition as they do in East Slavic cultures. If we compare a common expression that contains the word *svoj* in all Slavic languages as an example, the semantic differences among the languages become clear rather quickly. In Russian (and the respective Ukrainian and Belorussian variants), the sentence *On svoj chelovek* means "He is one of us." The word *svoj* places the person referenced within a larger group or collective. However, the same expressions in Czech, a West Slavic language, and Serbian, a South Slavic language, "*On je svůj člověk*" and "*On je svoj čovek*" mean "He is his own man" (which is what a Western European with some familiarity with Slavic languages would most likely have intuited). Here the word *svůj/svoj* refers to the individual and his ability to "make it on his own." Czech uses the word *naš* (our), as in *On je naš člověk* ("He is one of us," or "He is our man"), to refer to the person's affiliation with a larger group. East Slavic languages use *nash* as well, but the meaning is almost synonymous with *On svoj chelovek*. The Leda Russian/Czech dictionary translates the word *svoj* when it refers to a person as "*naš člověk*," not "*svůj*," even though the latter word certainly exists in Czech and is used to refer to ownership of some kind. Native speakers of Czech and Serbian have confirmed that the words *svoj* and *chuzhoj* (in their respective languages) do not interact in the same way as they do in Russian. Polish, also a West Slavic language, is closer to its East Slavic cousins than to Czech in this respect. The use of *svoj* is almost identical in Polish to its use in Russian. However, the use of *cudzy (chuzhoj)* is not and the two words are not considered direct opposites.[8] At the same time, I suspect that almost every native Russian speaker will confirm that at present these two words are intricately related and that the antonym for the word *svoj* is *chuzhoj*, and vice versa. In fact, most Russian dictionaries use the phrase *ne*

---

8   From private conversation with Anna Frajlich-Zajac, a Polish poet and retired lecturer in Polish language and literature at Columbia University.

svoj to define the word *chuzhoj* (something that dictionaries for other Slavic languages do not do).

At least three collections of idioms and proverbs that I have consulted, Vladimir Dal''s 1862 *Proverbs of the Russian People* (*Poslovitsy russkogo naroda*), A. Zhigulyev's 1958 *Russian Folk Proverbs and Sayings* (*Russkie narodnye poslovitsy i pogovorki*), and Sophia Lubensky's 1995 *Russian-English Dictionary of Idioms*, list entries that include both the words *svoj* and *chuzhoj* in opposition, with most, but not all, showing the "possession" usage of the words. Lubensky offers two examples. The first is: "Свои собаки грызутся (дерутся), чужая не подходи (не приставай)" (lit. "[Our] own dogs are gnawing [fighting] amongst themselves; a foreign/alien one should not approach [bother]"). Lubensky explains the meaning: mind your own business; keep your nose out of it. The second is: "В чужой монастырь со своим уставом не ходят" (lit. "One does not go to a foreign monastery with one's own rules"). Lubensky: when in Rome, do as the Romans do.

In Zhigulev's collection we can find literally dozens of examples, but I will limit myself to three: "Свои сухари лучше чужих пирогов" (One's own rusks are better than someone else's pies), "Чужие грехи пред очами, а свои за плечами" (Someone else's sins are right in front of your eyes while your own are behind your shoulders [forgotten, ignored]), "Чужую кровлю кроет, а своя течет" ([Someone] is fixing someone else's roof while his own is leaking). The first one establishes a common line of thought throughout the collection that one's own possessions/relatives are better than foreign ones or someone else's, even if they are of less quality or somehow less attractive. The other two advise one to stop worrying about other people's problems/sins and concentrate on one's own. Although the "one's own" pole of the opposition here does seem more valued, there is no reason to believe that these "other people/strangers" necessarily constitute a danger or threat.

Vladimir Dal' 's monumental work perhaps goes the furthest in proving that the two words work in opposition to one another. Dal' does not organize his book alphabetically as one would expect; instead, he creates "clusters" of general terms and sets of antonyms and synonyms under which he lists the proverbs and sayings that he feels correspond to them. Thus we find the headings *P' yanstvo* [Drunkenness], *Smekh—shutka—vesel' e* [Laughter—joking—merriment], *Zdorov' e—khvor'* [Health—illness], and, significantly, *Svoe—chuzhoe* [One's own—someone else's]. Under this last cluster we find full eighteen pages of entries, most of which contain both words of the opposition in a single saying or proverb. Some, however, do not contain either of the terms; Dal' presumably interpreted certain proverbs through the lens of the *svoj/chuzhoj* opposition.

Most of the sayings follow the pattern of "one's own" goods being preferable to "someone else's." Thus, we find the typical (and alliterative) "Своя рогожа чужой рожи дороже" (One's own bast matting is dearer than someone else's mug) and "Ешь чужие пироги, а свои (а свой хлеб) вперед береги!" (Eat someone else's pies, and keep your own (your bread) for later!). When the words are used to refer to people, there is often a sentiment of perplexity at the actions of one's own clan: "Что мне до чужих? Да пропадай хоть и свои!" (What do I care about strangers? First my own people need to take a hike!) and "Кому от чужих, а нам от своих" (Some people get it from strangers, while we get it from our own people). We also find the more nuanced "Не береги свое, береги чужое" (Don't watch out for your own goods, watch out for your brother's) and "Чужое береги, а свое бережется само" (Watch out for your brother's goods, and your own will take care of themselves). In these two instances, the foreign, alien component of the opposition seems to be valued at the very least as much as the more familiar one. The advice, contrary to what we see in Zhigulev, seems to be that someone else's goods need care as much as one's own.

In fact, as we see in Lubensky's list, the word *chuzhoj* was once neutral enough to translate at least one phrase from the Bible as "В чужом глазу сучок видим, а в своем (и) бревна не замечаем" (One sees the speck [the splinter, mote] in another's [one's brother's] eye and ignores the log [the plank] in his own). The word *chuzhoj* seems to have been almost synonymous at some point with the Russian word *blizhnii* (neighbor), as the above proverb is occasionally translated using this word as well. In the notes to Saltykov-Shchedrin's 1876 novel *The Golovlev Family* (*Gospoda Golovlevy*), we find the following translation: "У ближнего сучок в глазу видим, а у себя и бревна не замечаем" (We see the splinter in a neighbor's eye, but don't notice the log in our own), followed by the direct quote from the Gospel according to Matthew that uses the term *tvoi brat* (your brother), as in English: "Вынь прежде бревно из твоего глаза, и тогда увидишь, как вынуть сучок из глаза брата твоего" (Remove the log from your own eye first, then you will see how to remove the splinter from your brother's eye).

At the same time, the word *svoj*, when applied to a person, once referred primarily to a relation by marriage. Although the language has separate terms describing a relationship by blood (*rodstvo*) and a relationship by marriage (*svoistvo*), the distinction is often not very significant for many Russians. In general, Russians tend to overstate the closeness of a relationship. Even in the present day, a Russian will frequently refer to a first or even second cousin simply as *moi brat* (my brother) or *moya sestra* (my sister). Only later does one discover that the Russian is actually referring to his *dvoyurodnyi brat/dvoyurodnaya sestra* ("cousin" or "brother/sister once-removed"), not his *rodnoi brat/rodnaya sestra* ("full" or "blood brother/sister"). This cousin could be either his own or his wife's. O. N. Trubachev asserts that this tendency is a deep-rooted one among the Slavs. In his 1959 *A History of Slavic Terminology for Blood Relations* (*Istoriya slavyanskikh terminov rodstva*), Trubachev includes an entire chapter on *svoistvo*, in which he writes: "It turns out that a very far-reaching group of relatives, all the way from a man's full sister to his wife's very distant relatives, was called *svoi*; in other words, in the pre-modern period an analysis of the terminology does not suggest a clear division between a husband's relatives and his wife's" (90). Indeed, several terms for more "distant" relatives in Russian are formed from the word *svoj*—*svoyak, svoistvennik, svoyachenitsa* ("brother-in-law/general in-law," "cousin in-law/relative by wedlock," "sister-in-law"). In the instances involving a relation by blood or marriage, the antonym of the word *svoj*—*chuzhoj*—was in no way defamatory; it indicated the absence of such a relationship in someone vis-à-vis another person and nothing more.

To add to Trubachev's above statements, however, I would like to point out that at times people who were completely *unrelated* could also be considered *svoj chelovek*, a phenomenon to which the following memoir can attest. In Yankova's *Grandmother's Stories* mentioned earlier, the reader is assaulted with list upon list of relatives, the names of their estates, and the names of people whom they married within the nobility of old Moscow. Yankova describes a time, especially in her reminiscences of the eighteenth century, when almost everyone her family knew was *svoj chelovek* and the *chuzhie* were merely people with whom she had little or no contact.

Yankova's Moscow in this earlier portion of her memoirs is a place of very set social boundaries and delineations. The author spends her days visiting relatives and then describing to the reader exactly how she is related to them. A typical passage from her journal reads: "The Tatishchev's third house was flanked on one side by the Pashkovs' house and on the other by the Naryshkins'. My uncle Aleksei Evgrafovich lived here; he had married Marya Stepanovna Rzhevskaya, daughter of Stepan Matveevich, who had married the baroness Stroganova, Sofya Nikolaevna. Consequently, through the Stroganovs, she was related by marriage (*v svoistve*), although distantly, to the Tatishchevs" (48). The family histories of the people with whom Yankova associated were so intricately interwoven that in one case she writes of someone to whom she is actually doubly related ("Мы были все-таки и даже вдвойне свои," 195), in this instance through her father's grandmother and her mother's grandfather.

As one of the grande dames of Moscow high society, Yankova was in the enviable position of being able at times to bestow the designation of *svoj chelovek* on someone who was not only not related to her, but from an entirely different social stratum altogether. Significantly, the *very first* anecdote that Yankova relates in her memoirs involves just such a bestowment. On a basic level, the story serves as an introduction to an even grander dame, one Evpraksia Vasilievna Shepeleva, the author's paternal grandmother, but on another level it effectively depicts the allure of dubbing and being dubbed *svoj chelovek*. Shepeleva, while preparing for a *zvanyi obed* (dinner by invitation) in honor of one of her many relations by marriage, instructs her servants to invite the local priest's wife, a person usually outside the social circle of a member of the gentry. The priest's wife arrives, and Shepeleva jokingly admonishes her for never coming to visit. When the woman protests that she would not dare show up on the doorstep without an invitation, Shepeleva tells her she is being silly and is welcome anytime. Yankova describes the scene as the priest's wife hesitates in approaching the table in such august company: "And then it was time for dinner; the butler announced solemnly: 'Dinner is served.' As the hostess led Shuvalova [the guest of honor—J.G.] to the table by the hand, she saw that the priest's wife was merely standing there. Wishing to encourage her, she said, 'Come on, dear,[9] you're one of us (*svoj chelovek*); today do not wait for me to serve you. Take whatever catches your fancy'" (8). One gets the impression that of all the things Yankova's grandmother could have said to encourage the priest's wife, designating her *svoj chelovek*, especially in front of an important visitor, ranks at the top of the list in terms of respect and honor.

By the same token, the perceived revoking of this honor could prove embarrassing. The story involving Yankova's grandmother does not end with the priest's wife living happily ever after with her new clan; when the poor woman follows Shepeleva's instructions not to stand on ceremony, she is chastised for eating too much of the quality fish:

> "My dear, were you the one who ate all my fish?" Grandmother asked threateningly.
>
> "I did, my lady, your Excellency, it was definitely me, I'm guilty," muttered the priest's wife. "Stupid of me..."
>
> Grandmother and all her guests burst out laughing at the sight of her.
>
> "How in the world did it come to you to eat up all of this excellent fish?" the hostess asked laughing.

---

9 Shepeleva calls her *popad'ya* (priest's wife) in direct address, which is impossible to say in English. The tone is affectionate, however.

"I am sorry, my lady, your Excellency! You said I could go up to the table, you said that I was one of the group (*svoj chelovek*) and that I shouldn't stand on ceremony and that I should eat whatever took my fancy . . . I sat at the table, saw that a huge piece of fish was in front of me,— a good piece it looked to me, I decided to try it, and before I knew it, a few pieces here, a few swallows there, and all of a sudden, the fish was gone . . ."

Grandmother and the countess were guffawing even more than before; the guests added their laughter as well.

"Well, my dear, you've really done it this time, that's for sure. I need to thank you! I looked all over for this fish—and in one sitting she eats the whole thing! Did you think it was brought in for you? Really, my dear, you are a fool." (10)

Although this second half of the anecdote seems to portray Yankova's grandmother in a rather unflattering light, it is possible that she was not being totally serious. In this interpretation, the tale is a kind of welcoming to the club and to the gentle ribbing one was to expect from *svoi lyudi* (one's own people). If she was not joking, the story still reveals the powerful feelings of honor and subsequent humiliation, which surrounded the bestowment and revocation of the status. In either case, the anecdote, coming as it does on the first page of chapter one of Yankova's memoirs, introduces the reader to a world structured on the basis of the *svoj/chuzhoj* opposition. In this milieu of relative stability, everyone knew everyone else and ancient Moscow families like Shepeleva's were able to play with the designation *svoj* in any way it saw fit.

The above vignette (as well as Olga Yokoyama's thoughts on the wide scope of a Russian's clan) also supports Wladimir Weidle's view of the Russian family as especially elastic and organic. In the chapter "The Russian Soul" in his 1952 book *Russia: Absent and Present*, Weidle writes:

It is this close association of the erotic with family life, this fidelity of the family to its natural pre-human origins that chiefly distinguishes Russia from the West. The family remains, even now, a powerful institution in many western countries, especially in France; but there it is precisely as an *institution* that it commands respect and receives the protection of the law. It is something not so much given as required. A French family is founded as a new social cell, detached—one might even say severed—from the rest of society, and its members are so many citizens of a miniature State, the life of which is regulated by a constitution, an unwritten constitution but one well known to all. It is based on law rather than morals and on morals very much more than on primitive instinct anterior to reason. It has all the solidity of a well-built house, but not the elasticity, the power of self-renewal, that organic tissue possesses; whereas in Russia the principle of the family is organic, something vital—animal, if you will; it transcends the bounds of what is strictly the family and those of consanguinity in the more exact sense. In France, and to some extent throughout the western world, the family may be thought of in terms of common law; but in Russia common law itself has always tended to be superseded by human relations made in the image of the family. The family was never a self-enclosed unit; it expanded, gathered to its bosom those who were strangers to it by birth: servants, guests, often a whole group of friends and "relations" were allowed to share in its private life. [10] Such a notion as that of a "lackey", imported (like the word itself) from abroad, with the feeling of contempt that came to be associated with it, is entirely strange to Russian ideas; so much so indeed, that all kinds of poor relations and pensioners, former midwives and wet-nurses, retired children's maids and servants of all sorts whose working years were over, formed at all times, for the Russian family, a kind of frontier guard, the implied mission of which was to defend the family against all in the outer world that was too hard, too rigid and too unhomely. (133)

Indeed, this organic flexibility can be found in many Russian families to this day, although I would add that someone most likely came to a decision to include these wet-nurses and retired maids into the circle; it didn't just happen. What has changed, however, is the threat to which Weidle refers that is posed by this "outer world." In the early eighteenth century when Yankova's grandmother lived, the threat seems at first glance to have been rather negligible. It was not long, however, before cracks began to appear in the old nobility's armor and Moscow's preeminence began to wane.

---

10 Some Russian terms for strangers are even familial—"some guy/lady on the street" would be rendered as *dyadya/tetka* (uncle/auntie).

Peter the Great issued his Table of Ranks in January of 1722 to the dismay of many among the ancient Moscow families. The Table made it possible for men from all sorts of backgrounds to enter the ranks of the nobility. Marc Raeff, in his 1966 *Origins of the Russian Intelligentsia*, writes on the subject:

> Not until the 1840 s did the nobleman find new, promising fields in economic enterprise and the professions. Until almost the end of the imperial regime, public recognition and official reward in these new fields of endeavor came in the shape of ranks and titles from the Table of Ranks. The professional man of non-noble origin took advantage of this situation to further his career as well as the status of his family; through the Table of Ranks he could first become associated with the elite and eventually join the nobility. Not until the last quarter of the nineteenth century did the hierarchy of the Table of Ranks cease to be the principal gauge of success for the professional man, as well as for the state servant. (118–119)

Coupled with what the Moscow nobility perceived as an assault on their primacy in Russian society and on their influence over the politics of old Muscovy came the rise of St. Petersburg as the new power center in the country. As Yankova's memoirs progress, the author makes more and more references to people she knows moving from Moscow to St. Petersburg:

> In my memory there were only two grandee houses like the Dolgorukovs' and the Apraksins'. This was at a time when there were still many distinguished and wealthy people in Moscow, when people had the means and knew how to live grandly and merrily and enjoyed doing so. Nowadays there is not a glimmer of what once was: The prominent and wealthy are all in Petersburg. Anyone living out his days in Moscow has either become obsolete or lost his fortune. They sit at home quietly, with little money, and live not like a gentleman, as they used to, but like a member of the petty bourgeoisie, keeping to themselves. Everything is more expensive and luxurious, and their needs have increased, but they do not have the means to keep up. They live not as they want to, but as they are able to. If we raised our ancestors and let them take a look at Moscow, they would gasp in shock at the sight... No question, Moscow

has become shallow and its residents are petty, even if there are lots of them. Perhaps there are good names still around, but the people are gone. They don't live up to their names. (151)

Via the Table of Ranks, Peter was able to force the old Moscow families to serve in St. Petersburg, miles and miles away from their beloved country estates, which constituted worlds of their own. On these estates, the families themselves decided how to govern and what the pecking order was, with little interference from the outside world. They knew exactly who was *svoj chelovek*. As the eighteenth century unfolded and the traditional, estate-owning noble families became less and less influential, they could no longer rely on the once tightly woven safety net of blood lines, kinship by marriage, and family name. As for the people who "don't live up to their names," Yankova may have been referring to certain members of two very old Moscow families that are mentioned constantly throughout the memoirs. Both Petr Tolstoy and Mikhail Dolgorukov and their descendants became strong supporters of Peter's reforms, much to the consternation of their Moscow relations.

In the early eighteenth century, the Moscow families still retained their clout, a clout that they used as well as they could to thwart Peter and the city that bears his name. In their opinion, Peter spent too much money on wars waged for no real reason and on a navy that, in their view, would bring little to no benefit to the country. They also believed he spent too much time associating with foreigners, mostly Germans in their special settlements in Petersburg. Indeed, Peter's new city on the Neva aroused very strong feelings among the entrenched Moscow elite. L. Jay Oliva, in his book *Russia in the Era of Peter the Great*, writes:

> For the old metropolitan nobility then, Saint Petersburg was the city of the "fledglings" and the "accidental men" who merited none of the power and preference lavished upon them by the Tsar, the city of the infamous Table of Ranks, which lifted the lowly over the heads of the deserving, the city of the foreigners, of high prices and enforced building of new palaces, of miserable living conditions far from their cherished estates in the environs of Moscow. Petersburg was to them a premeditated assault on Moscow and all that it had meant to these ancient service families. (160)

It was not just the Moscow elite that resisted the rise of Petersburg and the reforms that came with it. Peter's reign also saw a number of popular revolts, including one in Astrakhan, one on the Volga led by disgruntled Bashkirs, and one in the Don valley mounted by Cossacks. The new system united the *narod* (the people) with the Moscow nobles in their longing for a Russia that had once been, a time when a Moscow noblewoman was sure enough of her status to include a priest's wife in her inner circle and to make fun of her in jest.

As the century progressed and the Moscow elite's control over the *svoj/chuzhoj* opposition began to slip, the latter component of the concept began to be applied on a wider scale. We see the ethnic sphere of the *svoj/chuzhoj* opposition of which Ivanov and Toporov spoke begin to surface and, in essence, remain integral to Russians' view of the world from then on. Russified Germans became *chuzhie*, as did the entire city of St. Petersburg, with its Western name and architecture and its cosmopolitan makeup. As the lesser provincial nobility, one of the few groups that supported Peter's reforms, began to take positions on par or above those usually held by the ancient Moscow families, less and less attention was paid to the system of relations Yankova relied on so heavily in her memoirs to make sense of the developments in the world of her time.

Chapter 10 of *Grandmother's Stories* effectively conveys the loss of influence and prestige of the once all-powerful city of Moscow. And, as in chapter 1, Yankova begins with an anecdote involving the application of the label *svoj*. Arriving in the city for the first time after the Great Fire of 1812, Yankova describes not only the physical destruction of her beloved Moscow, once full of *svoi lyudi*, but also the perceived violation of expected behavior for someone designated as such:

> My brothers' houses stood intact and we decided to stay at my brother Nikolai Petrovich's place. He had invited us and my sister-in-law had tried to send word of our arrival to the house since they were staying in Pokrovsky and their house on Znamenka was empty. So, after arriving in Moscow, we headed straight for Znamenka.
>
> A servant who lived in the house emerged and told us: "I don't dare receive you because as the masters were leaving they did not leave orders to receive anyone."
>
> I told him: "But I'm Nikolai Petrovich's sister, and my sister-in-law tried to send word that we would stay here for a while until we rent a house."
>
> "I don't dare, my lady, and I have received no letters."
>
> This was truly insulting to me.

"Well, if our own (*svoi*) won't receive us," Dmitry Aleksandrovich said, "let's go to a stranger's (*k chuzhim*), to my friend Dmitry Petrovich Shcherbachev's house. Even though he is not family, he will welcome us with open arms; I guarantee it." (199)

Yankova here shows the reader that more than the physical structures of ancient Moscow have been compromised; her trust in the *svoj/chuzhoj* system has also been damaged.

The word *chuzhoj*, however, has not taken on negative connotations by this point. The phrase, "поедем к чужим, к моему другу . . ." (let's go to a stranger's, to my friend's . . .) shows both the difficulty in explaining the word *chuzhoj* to a non-Russian speaker and the relative neutrality of its meaning at the time. The usual English translations given for the word when it refers to a person—"stranger," "alien," "outsider"—make little sense before the explanatory ". . . to my friend's." For an English speaker, what kind of a stranger can also be a friend? But for Russians, at least of this time, this type of relationship was rather common. For Dmitrii Aleksandrovich, this unsuspecting host is indeed a friend, but he is decidedly not *svoj chelovek*. He is *chuzhoj*, but no harm done.

Yankova puts a slightly different spin on the matter, however. As if to justify her and her husband's resorting to staying with *chuzhie lyudi*, Yankova follows with a rather lengthy description of how wonderful this Shcherbachev was and how close he and her husband had become: "Shcherbachev was a friend of Dmitrii Aleksandrovich from the corps. He was always very friendly with him and loved him like a brother. He was a very kind person, affectionate and cordial to everyone, and was like the closest of relatives to us. He was prepared to grant most any request or favor" (199). Again, Yankova evaluates a person's worth by saying how much he was like a member of the family.

Yankova was not unique in her interpretation of who was *svoj* at the time. In Mikhail Gershenzon's *Griboedov's Moscow* (*Griboedovskaya Moskva*), published in 1914, the author searches Moscow high society of a century before for possible prototypes for the characters in Griboedov's play. He delves particularly deeply into the life of Marya Ivanovna Rimskaya-Korsakova, a relative of Yankova's and another important figure in Moscow society of the time. Because Marya Ivanovna kept detailed records of the minutiae of her life and was an exceptionally prolific letter-writer, Gershenzon is able to convey to his reader a vivid picture of what her day-to-day life was like. Again, much of the details about this noblewoman and her adventures in Moscow society are relayed through the lens of the *svoj/chuzhoj* opposition. At times Gershenzon even seems to go out of his way to explain who exactly qualifies as *svoj*, as if early twentieth-century readers would need the clarification. The following excerpts are in Gershenzon's words, although he strove as much as possible to keep to Marya Ivanovna's style and wording.[11]

The first anecdote involving the opposition shows the reader that not everyone who lived in the house was regarded as *svoj*: "The house was occupied besides one's own (*svoikh*), by several old ladies, Marya Timofeevna and some others, and a blind old man named Petr Ivanovich—'my team of invalids,' as Marya Ivanovna referred to them, not without affection" (60). It is not clear to whom Gershenzon believes the word *svoj* refers in this anecdote. Is he reserving it merely for Marya Ivanovna's direct relatives? It seems that in this household the blind old man and the old women could certainly qualify as *svoi*, but in this case they are not included in the privileged grouping. A direct quote from Marya Ivanovna later in Gershenzon's tale, however, may shed some light on the matter. In telling her son Grisha to allow Marya Timofeevna to read a particularly personal letter of hers, Marya Ivanovna writes: "I know that she will go to her grave with this, and my trust will serve her instead of medicine" (107). Marya Ivanovna's entrusting of this personal letter to Marfa could be her way of bringing her into the group of *svoi lyudi* in the household. Gershenzon, after all, was sufficiently surprised to include this anecdote; he prefaces the above quote with the following words: "And she [Marya Ivanovna—J.G.] even allowed Grisha to let her favorite hanger-on, Marfa Timofeevna, read the letter" (107).

One did not have to be a hanger-on or a member of an old Moscow family, however, to make it into the ranks of the *svoi*. In fact, even a Jew could qualify:

> Marya Ivanovna rises early, at seven, sometimes six o'clock. Only if she returned home late from a ball the previous night would she sleep in until nine. After saying her morning prayers, she enters the drawing room to have tea with her confidante, the chamber-maid Dunyashka. As soon as she finishes her tea, the ministers enter with their reports. The head minister is Yakov Ivanovich Rosenberg; he has lived in the house for a long time and is fully one of the family [*svoj chelovek*]. (61)

---

11 Vera Proskurina writes in the commentary to her 1998 book *Mikhail Gershenzon: His Life and Myth*: "Gershenzon was careful to reproduce the idiosyncrasies of M. I. Rimskaya-Korsakova's epistolary language and avoided conforming to the norms of orthography and punctuation" (365).

Marya Ivanovna's household indeed bears resemblance to the organic Russian family, which Wladimir Weidle praised in his *Russia: Absent and Present*.

A few pages later, Gershenzon explains who else enjoyed the *svoj* status in Marya Ivanovna's household: "But usually Marya Ivanovna eats lunch at home with her people (*so svoimi*), in other words with the servants and two or three friends" (66). Here the hired help and the high nobility dine together side by side as *svoi lyudi* (all one family), a phenomenon that may have moved Gershenzon to elaborate (note the "in other words," which he adds).

For all the benefits that the *svoj* label bestowed on its recipients, the following excerpt serves as evidence that those who had not achieved the status were not necessarily viewed negatively: "But guests do not call every morning. If there are no strangers (*net chuzhikh*) at the door, Marya Ivanovna is out and about even before lunch" (66). In this anecdote, the word *chuzhoj* merely indicates a guest, a person who is not in this inner circle of close confidants; it has yet to acquire any pejorative connotations and it is still incorrect to translate as "strangers" or even "outsiders" into English.

As the nineteenth century progressed, however, the bonds of kinship began to fray. Especially in the second half of her memoir, we see Yankova become increasingly distressed as the years pass and the *svoj/chuzhoj* opposition becomes more and more disregarded. The author gripes about many of the typical things one gripes about in old age— new styles of clothing, transport, and the behavior of the young— but the most expressive language is reserved for people who fail to respect the bonds of *rodstvo* and *svoistvo*: "Nowadays kinship is not taken seriously at all; how quickly if you're not full brothers or sisters, then you're not related: people marry their cousins; soon the time will come perhaps when sisters will marry their full brothers and uncles will marry their full nieces! No, in our day if you could say you were related to someone, even distantly, you were not strangers (*ne chuzhie*), but one of the clan (*svoi lyudi*)—a relation by marriage" (195).

The memoirist is a person whose entire worldview and sense of worth were determined by relatives and close confidants and the traditions and behaviors that everyone, at least at some point, followed and respected. And it is clear that while Yankova does not understand or accept the city of St. Petersburg and its new nobility, which have begun to gain influence and prestige, there is no sense that she regards them as sinister or evil. They are, for her, merely not worth associating with. In her musings about what her ancestors would think if they could see the Moscow of the early nineteenth century, we see her more bewildered and hurt than resentful or frightened.

Aleksandr Pushkin's works provide ample evidence that he too was troubled by the situation at hand. Russia's most revered poet in some ways personifies the conflict Yankova had written so much about. Pushkin descended on his father's side from an ancient noble family and was fiercely proud of his ancestry. In his 1989 book *Puškin: Literature and Social Ideas*, Sam Driver writes:

> On his father's side Puškin traces his ancestry back to the thirteenth century, to a certain Prussian nobleman, Radša (or Rača), who came to Russia in the reign of Alexander Nevskij (1220–1263). The family, if its claims are correct, is thus one of the oldest among those recorded in Europe; the Musins, Mjatlevs, Buturlins, and other notable families are also descended from Radša. The family claim was made in 1686; the first mention of the surname was in the seventh generation (*koleno*) from Radša, a certain Grigorij Puška. From this Gregory Puška, who lived at the end of the fourteenth and the beginning of the fifteenth century, the line descended. (21)

However, Pushkin's mother, a distant cousin of her husband's, was the granddaughter of an African who had been brought from Istanbul as a gift for Peter the Great. Pushkin's great-grandfather made his way up the ranks from lackey to valet to personal secretary and eventually, after a stint in a Parisian military academy, to general. In their introduction to the 2006 collection *Under the Sky of My Africa*, Catherine Theimer Nepomnyashchy and Ludmilla A. Trigos write:

> Roughly in the year 1705, a young African boy, acquired from the seraglio of the Turkish sultan by the Russian envoy in Constantinople (Istanbul), was transported to Russia as a gift to Tsar Peter the Great, who was known for his love of the exotic and the odd. As the vagaries of history would have it, this child, later known as Abram Petrovich Gannibal, was to become the godson of the ruler of the largest contiguous empire on earth, travel from one end of Europe to the other and across the huge expanses of Russia into Asia almost to the Chinese border, and survive six of Peter's successors to die at a ripe old age, having attained the rank of general and the status of Russian nobility. Most important, he was to become the great-grandfather of Russia's greatest national poet, Alexander Pushkin. (3)

Despite, or perhaps precisely because of, this mixture of ancient Russian noble blood with a distinctly foreign ancestor, who had to work hard to advance his career, Pushkin became keenly aware of the inner workings of the social scene and just how success could be achieved. Certainly, this mixed lineage complicated the *svoj/chuzhoj* issue for the writer, whom many viewed as an outsider because of his African blood. The young poet attended the prestigious Lycée in Tsarskoe Selo, entry to which was largely determined by proof of lineage from the ancient Moscow families. There Pushkin absorbed the elitist but rather liberal political atmosphere of his peers and teachers. Liberal leanings were limited, however, as Driver points out: "The liberality of opinion, however, was primarily conditioned by the opposition of the aristocracy (here in the sense of the old families) to the autocracy and its creature, the 'service nobility'" (24).

As Driver describes it, Pushkin's years at the Lycée were indeed largely occupied by this strained interaction between the sons of the old Moscow families and the newer Petersburg elite, which included, in the eyes of nobles whose blood lines were older than the Romanovs, the royal family as well. To the consternation of I. I. Pushchin, one of Pushkin's friends at the Lycee and also a descendant of an ancient Moscow line of nobles, the Empress Maria Fedorovna in particular no longer held the older blood lines in such high regard. Driver quotes Pushchin (translation Driver's): "Aleksandr . . . intended to educate us with his brothers, Grand Dukes Nikolaj and Mixail, who were almost our peers in age: but the Empress Marija Fedorovna opposed this, finding too democratic and improper the bringing together of her sons, Imperial personages, with us, plebeians" (24).

As we can see, the snobbery ran both ways. Pushkin, although clearly perceived as on the side of the older Moscow families, occasionally encountered criticism from his group of *svoi* when he was seen laughing it up with court favorites. Driver writes that this behavior, in the eyes of the Moscow nobles, was perceived as a betrayal of their social caste. I would add that the betrayal was made all the more threatening given the fact that the nobles' cool self-assurance in their status in Russian society was seriously faltering.

The fate of the ancient Moscow families occupied Pushkin for a large part of his literary career. Many of his essays of the 1830s touch on the subject, and one piece of non-fiction in particular, *A Journey from Moscow to Petersburg* (*Puteshestvie iz Moskvy v Peterburg*) includes a chapter, entitled "Moscow" (added in 1835), which echoes many of Yankova's complaints about the sorry state of a once grand city. The chapter begins by invoking the author of the work to which the title of Pushkin's own journey alludes: Aleksandr Radishchev. Radishchev's *A Journey from Petersburg to Moscow* (*Puteshestvie iz Peterburga v Moskvu*), published anonymously in 1790, called attention to, among other things, the plight of the Russian serf. Pushkin, in turn, uses his journey to remind us of the plight of the fallen Moscow nobleman. Called out for special praise is the nobleman's former independence from the dictates of St. Petersburg, an independence that allowed for their, according to Pushkin, "innocent idiosyncrasies" ("невинные странности"). In remarkably wistful tones, Pushkin describes a more care free time, when anyone who was anyone descended on Moscow for the winter, grandiose feasts and balls were thrown, and "все были свои" (all were among their own): "Они жили по-своему, забавлялись как хотели, мало заботясь о мнении ближнего" (They lived in their own way [according to their own?—J.G.], entertained as they wished, and cared little about the opinion of neighbors, 188). Is it possible that Pushkin, writing here in the 1830s, wanted to use *chuzhoj* in this sentence but the word had already acquired too sinister a connotation?

Especially after 1812, as Pushkin notes, times had changed, and Moscow and its inhabitants looked quite a bit different:

> Nowadays subdued Moscow contains enormous boyar houses standing sadly between a large courtyard, overgrown with weeds, and a neglected and unkempt orchard. A tailor, who pays the owner thirty rubles a month for his apartment, hangs up his sign, and there it is, protruding from under the gilded family crest. The magnificent bel étage is rented out to a French school teacher for a boarding school—and thank God it's only that! A notice has been nailed to all the gates announcing that the house is for sale or rent, but no one buys and no one rents. The streets are dead; rare is the sound of a carriage's wheels on the bridge; the young ladies run to the windows whenever the chief of police rides by with his Cossacks. The villages surrounding Moscow are empty and mournful as well. (188)

Naturally, Pushkin and many of his contemporaries from his class and background blamed Peter and his perceived hatred for Moscow for the fall in prestige of the city and its unique way of life. According to Pushkin, Peter saw nothing but superstition and prejudice in the former capital, and the emperor's battle against them placed him squarely at odds with the ancient Moscow families: "Peter I did not like Moscow, where he was confronted at every step with memories of revolts and executions, the deeply ingrained roots of the old ways and stubborn resistance born of superstition and prejudice" (189).

In his own "Journey," Pushkin goes to great lengths to praise the Russian peasant and uses Denis Fonvizin's thoughts from a trip to France to prove that his condition is not nearly as grievous as that of a French field worker or English factory laborer. Indeed, according to Pushkin, the Russian peasant is living better by the day: "The fate of the peasant is improving day by day as far as enlightenment spreads . . . The welfare of the peasants is closely linked with the welfare of the landowners; this is obvious to anyone" (200). Pushkin here stresses the mutual interaction and dependence of the old nobility and the peasants. The two groups were of different social classes, of course, but in a way were more *svoi* to each other (or had the potential to be) than to the new service nobility, to the foreigners who were inundating St. Petersburg and making inroads in Moscow, or to a third estate, the *raznochintsy*, who were being tapped to fill various administrative positions throughout the country.[12]

Although the term is most often attached (approvingly) to the radical literary critics of the later nineteenth century, people like Vissarion Belinsky, Nikolai Chernyshevsky, and Nikolai Dobrolyubov, who indeed rose from social obscurity to become very influential figures in Russian society, Driver writes that in Pushkin's time the word did not have such positive associations: "While the social code assumed a pro forma, desultory performance in the part of the noble, the men 'of various ranks' recognized that their performance and advancement would come through assiduousness and loyalty to the bureaucracy and ultimately to the autocracy. Whatever their role later in the century, they were perceived by Puškin's class as something other than gentlemen, as something close to toadies, or worse" (16).

Peter the Great had begun turning to these *raznochintsy* to staff positions that either were too numerous to be filled with only noblemen or that the noblemen deemed beneath them.[13] By the early nineteenth century, this motley group

---

12 David K. Danow, in the *Handbook of Russian Literature*, defines the *raznochintsy* as "A social term referring to 'people of diverse rank' or 'people of no particular estate.' These were a new breed within Russian society of mixed background below the gentry, including sons of clergy who did not follow the calling of their fathers, offspring of petty officials and of impoverished noblemen, and individuals from the masses, who made their way, through education and persistent effort. Having emerged from provincial, clerical, and petty-bourgeois squalor, they rose with difficulty from poverty and social obscurity, frequently by tutoring, doing translation work, or through journalism" (363).

13 Marc Raeff, in the chapter "The State and Service in the Eighteenth Century" explains: "The nobles preferred to go into the new army and navy rather than into the administrative bureaus, and Peter was only too glad to encourage this trend, for military needs took precedence. In the administration, a higher level of literacy was needed, even for the lower positions, while the positions of responsibility and leadership required talents that could not be acquired through apprenticeship and experience alone. It was not surprising, therefore, that the government

had become such a social and political force that no one, including the leading writers of the time, could ignore them. The writer who in part moved Pushkin to remark on the fall of the Moscow he once knew and loved was Aleksandr Griboedov, who, roughly a decade earlier, had finished work on his masterpiece drama *Woe from Wit*. Griboedov was also deeply interested in the interaction of the old Moscow families with the *raznochintsy* and the newer nobility of the capital. In my next chapter, I will read the author's works, particularly *Woe from Wit*, from the point of view of the *svoj/chuzhoj* opposition. I will show how this piece of literature, although extremely well-received in manuscript form, also moved Griboedov's Moscow relations to accuse him of betraying his clan—in the context of this project a far from innocuous charge.

---

also turned to social groups outside the nobility proper to staff the various offices created in the process of modernizing and westernizing the Russian state. The main source were the *raznochintsy*—i.e. children of the clergy, with a sprinkling of sons of merchants, soldiers, and other non-noble free men" (52).

Chapter Two

Making Svoj/Chuzhoj Divisive in Aleksandr Griboedov's "Woe from Wit"

For generations, Russian elementary school pupils have read and memorized Aleksandr Griboedov's nineteenth-century masterpiece, *Woe from Wit* (*Gore ot uma*). The play is still part of the Russian school curriculum. Pushkin, who greatly respected and admired Griboedov, referring to him as a "true talent" in correspondence with the writer A. A. Bestuzhev, predicted in the same letter that half of the lines from *Woe from Wit* would enter common parlance. Pushkin was right, in part because he himself made use of many of Griboedov's turns of phrase in his own work, as did, in later years, Dostoevsky, Chekhov, Blok, Tsvetaeva, and Pasternak. This fact and the aphoristic nature of many of the comedy's lines have resulted in Griboedov becoming one of the most quoted of all Russian authors, second only to Pushkin himself. N. S. Ashukin's collection of most quoted expressions (*krylatye slova*) in Russian literature lists ninety-seven for Pushkin and fifty-seven for Griboedov, followed by Gogol (fifty-three) and I. A. Krylov (forty-seven). None of the authors popular in the West, such as Chekhov or Dostoevsky, even comes close (twenty-one and eight, respectively).

Of Griboedov's literary admirers, Blok perhaps went the furthest in his praise of the man. In his 1907 article "On Drama" ("O drame"), the author describes *Woe from Wit* as the "most magnificent creation in all our literature." A. Lebedev, in his 1980 book *Griboedov*, adds: "There was a time (right before 1917), when Griboedov became an especially important and intimate figure for Blok. At the time he believed that Griboedov was, for him, 'dearer than Pushkin'" (79). Readers of Mikhail Bulgakov's enormously popular *The Master and Margarita* (*Master i Margarita*, 1928–1940) will remember that much of the action in the novel takes place at Griboedov House, the restaurant-cum-headquarters of the Writers' Union in Moscow. In 1923, Soviet authorities showed their affection for the author by renaming the Ekaterininsky Canal, one of three major canals flowing through St. Petersburg, in his honor. Griboedov's appeal did not end with the collapse of the Soviet Union. In 1993, the A. S. Griboedov Institute of International Law and Economics was established in Moscow.

Despite Griboedov's popularity at home, his name is almost completely unknown to the Western reader. The conventional explanation for the West's ignorance of a major work like *Woe from Wit* points to the particularly rich and colloquial Russian that Griboedov used in the play. Translations of the work into English (or into most any language for that matter) usually sound flat and uninspired. In his 1985 book *Russian Drama: from its Beginnings to the Age of Pushkin*, Simon Karlinsky writes of the play (he prefers the translation of the title *The Misfortune of Being Clever*, which he compresses to *TMoBC*):

> Defying all translators, the text of the play is as idiomatic as the title. A blend of uproarious humor and hauntingly subtle verbal music in the original Russian, *TMoBC* is the ultimate proof that the art of literature is on its basic level the art of words. Griboedov's art is addressed to those who can understand his words instantly in all their finest shadings and ambiguities. *Some knowledge of Russian is no help at all*: students at Western universities who know enough of the language to read Turgenev or Akhmatova in the original shrug their shoulders at lines and passages in Griboedov that make native speakers gasp in awed wonder or slap their thighs in mirth. Nor has there yet been a translation into any language that can convey to people in other countries why this play is such a miracle of wit and verbal precision, though the Polish one by Julian Tuwim came close. (278)

I agree that the language of the play can definitely prove quite difficult for non-native Russian speakers, and in chapter 3, I return to Karlinsky's line about the play being written more for those "who can understand his words instantly." I would only add that apart from the words of the text, the social setting of the play eludes a non-native reader as well; in particular, the functioning of the *svoj/*

chuzhoj opposition at the time the work was written. This specific aspect of the work is crucial to a full understanding of it.

This chapter begins with a discussion of Griboedov's family background and of the society to which he belonged. These two factors affected his representation of the *svoj/chuzhoj* opposition in *Woe from Wit*. A close reading of certain scenes of the play follows, with special attention paid to the ways in which Griboedov employs the terms and concepts of *svoj* and *chuzhoj*. For I would like to propose several slightly non-traditional interpretations of some of the "fine shadings and ambiguities," which Karlinsky mentions as present in Griboedov's work, in the hope that by the end of the chapter the reader will understand the social and linguistic volatility in which the writer was operating and which he was reflecting. I will show that this volatility affected not only the content of the play but the very meaning of the words themselves; the shift in the way in which the words interacted with each other solidified the play's status as a literary work vital to the understanding of Russian culture.

The early nineteenth century marked a period of instability for the Russian literary language as well as for its upper-class society. In 1803, Admiral A. S. Shishkov published *A Treatise on the Old and New Style of the Russian Language* (*Rassuzhdenie o starom i novom sloge rossiiskogo yazyka*). In this work, Shishkov advocated retaining the purity of the Russian language and resisting what he believed to be unnecessary influence from French.[14] Shishkov wished to adhere to the idea of the three styles of language expressed by Lomonosov in the eighteenth century.[15] N. M. Karamzin's supporters had founded the short-lived but influential Arzamas literary circle in part to ridicule the Beseda literary group, which Shishkov had founded. Though not a member of either of these literary groups, Griboedov was more in line with the ideas of the Beseda circle

---

14 William Mills Todd III writes in his 1976 book *The Familiar Letter as a Literary Genre in the Age of Pushkin*: "In it [the treatise—J.G.] and subsequent articles the arch-conservative Shishkov took issue with the Sentimentalist, Karamzinian reforms of the language and defended Church Slavonic as the basis of the literary language and of Russian civilization. Specifically, he objected to periphrastic avoidance of concrete imagery, calques from French, and the loss of synonyms from various stylistic levels, which resulted from the use of a single style by Karamzin's imitators" (47).

15 Lomonosov identified three styles in the Russian language—high, middle, and low. "The structure of each style was defined by the relationship of Slavonic to Russian forms. Lomonosov assigned strictly defined genres to each style. Heroic poems, odes, and ceremonial speeches on important themes were to be written in the high style. The middle style was to be used for friendly verse epistles, satires, eclogues, elegies. . . . Comedies, humorous epigrams, songs, familiar epistles, and accounts of ordinary affairs were to be written in the low style." See V. V. Vinogradov, *Istoriia slov* (Moscow: Tolk, 1994), 58.

and those who advocated a more conservative approach to the Russian literary language.

The language of *Woe from Wit* has been praised as a masterful representation of the idiosyncratic, often archaic, spoken Russian, which the Moscow upper class in particular used in the 1810s and 1820s. In addition to its language, the play is often praised as the first representation of the *lishnii chelovek* (superfluous man) in Russian literature.[16] Although there is no shortage of examples of heroes in world literature who felt the odd man out, not fitting in society (Don Quixote, Childe Harold, Adolphe), Russian literature seems to have more than its fair share of such figures. Nineteenth-century Russian literary critics took the term "superfluous man" from the title of a work by Ivan Turgenev, *The Diary of a Superfluous Man* (*Dnevnik lishnego cheloveka*), published in 1850. The term was then retroactively applied to a whole host of literary figures that had come earlier. Aleksandr Chatsky, the protagonist of Griboedov's *Woe from Wit*, is usually regarded as the progenitor of a long line of such men in Russian literature, and naturally much has been written on why Chatsky has become superfluous (*lishnii* literally means "extra" or "spare"). Literary critics most often concentrate on interpreting Chatsky's (and Griboedov's) views on the political issues of the day, namely the rights of serfs, explaining his status as superfluous by pointing to his alleged radicalism. What interests me more, however, is not how Chatsky became superfluous but how much and why he has become *alien* or even *dangerous*[17] to the social milieu in which he was raised.

Such a discussion is not possible without an investigation into the changing society in which Aleksandr Griboedov was raised. The writer was born in Moscow in 1795 into an ancient but impoverished noble family. In his 1929 article "The Sociology of 'Woe from Wit'" ("Sotsiologiya 'Gorya ot uma'"), N. K. Piksanov writes: "The Griboedovs came from an ancient noble family: their lineage can be traced to the sixteenth century. Griboedovs served in the guards and were military commanders. They were related to many eminent families: the Odoevskys, the Naryshkins, and the Paskeviches" (264).[18] Griboedov's

---

16 A. Anikin, "Tema lishnego cheloveka v russkoi klassike," 2, https://www.portal-slovo.ru/philology/37141.php?ELEMENT_ID=37141&PAGEN_1=2.
17 In their most heated exchange, Famusov refers to Chatsky as an "опасный человек" (dangerous man, act 2, scene 2)
18 Grandmother Yankova was also related to one degree or another to all of these families. Although many have suggested that Griboedov's ancestors actually came from Poland (with the last name written Grzibovski and then corrupted into Griboedov), others, including the scholars B. P. Nikolaev, G. D. Ovchinnikov, and E. V. Tsymbal question this view. They state, in their article From the Family History of the Griboedovs ("Iz istorii sem'i Griboedovykh"), that the Griboedov name can be found in Russian history in Novgorod as early as 1503 and

uncle, Aleksei Fedorovich Griboedov, was famous for his lavish balls at which all of Moscow could be found in attendance. Again demonstrating the relatively closed society in which the old Moscow clans traveled, Griboedov's mother— well-known for her sharp tongue and acerbic wit— was herself a distant relative of her husband's. Her maiden name: Griboedova.

From an early age, Griboedov, like Pushkin, became well aware of the differences between his people and the parvenus of various backgrounds with whom he studied at the prestigious *Moskovsky blagorodnyi universitetsky pansion* (Moscow University Pension for the Sons of the Nobility). Piksanov points out that the sons of old families like Griboedovs's, who even wore a different color uniform from that of the *raznochintsy*, would often rent out parts of their Moscow mansions to their less socially prominent but affluent classmates. Although Griboedov himself was not as wealthy as many of his social peers, some of whom would arrive in the city for the school term with an entire retinue of servants and lackeys, he did possess the cachet of an impressive family history. The sense of entitlement instilled in these noble sons also affected their interaction with their school teachers, who were more often than not also *raznochintsy*, usually the sons of priests (*popovichi*).

Nobles of the older Moscow line came into conflict not only with the *raznochintsy*; there were also the Petersburg grandees (*vel' mozhi*) or service nobility (*znat'*) with whom to contend. These men had acquired noble status through their exemplary service to the tsar. As Grandmother Yankova complained in her memoirs, some of these "grandees" were actually from old Moscow families but had gone over to Peter's side a century before. Piksanov's article on the sociology of *Woe from Wit* shows the contempt in which the Moscow families held this new Petersburg noble: "Even Prince P. A. Vyazemsky, a representative of the ancient line, felt alien and hostile to the grandees. He writes to Pushkin in 1829: 'We will not go to see the grandee, who will receive us on equal footing with the scoundrels, Bulgarin, and other scum of the public body'" (289).

This contempt was echoed by the poet Mikhail Lermontov, who composed his *Death of a Poet* (*Smert' poeta*) on the occasion of Pushkin's death in 1837. The poem makes reference to Pushkin's ancient lineage and the newer, less "real" Petersburg line of nobles:

---

make the case that the Polish version of provenance stems from the fashion of the time among Moscow nobles of claiming foreign ancestry. See "Iz istorii sem'i Griboedovykh," in *A. S. Griboedov: Materialy k biografii* (Leningrad: Nauka, 1989), 76–92, http://feb-web.ru/feb/griboed/critics/fom89/str_76.htm?cmd=p.

А Вы, надменные потомки
Известной подлостью прославленных отцов,
Пятою рабскою поправшие обломки
Игрою счастия обиженных родов!
Вы, жадною толпой стоящие у трона,
Свободы, гения и славы палачи!..

And you, you haughty ones, descendants
Of forebears known for shallowness of trait,
Who trample under slavery's heel the remnants
Of generations scarred by whim of fate!
You stand before the throne, a horde of greedy misers,
Who freedom, genius, honour, seek to kill![19]

Piksanov sums up the tension that existed between people like Lermontov, Pushkin, Griboedov, and Vyazemsky and the representatives of the service nobility, to which he refers below as the *znat'*:

> In all of these statements, a primordial enmity on the part of the ancestral, middling, cultured nobility of the capital (usually of modest means or having lost their fortune) towards this new service nobility emerges, an enmity that intensified in Griboedov's time. As a rule, these "remnants of clans insulted by fortune's whims" held the extravagantly wealthy and powerful set of tycoons in contempt. This service nobility had come into being in the eighteenth century through the favoritism shown by the empresses.
>
> It is precisely this middling cultured nobility of the capital to which Griboedov belonged as well. His noble ancestry was ancient. He had many family connections in the new service nobility. But the Griboedovs themselves did not belong to the new service nobility. The family's financial state was in ruins; Griboedov often was in need of money and at an early age was forced to serve. But he served the tsar "so that I had a way to feed my children." On a societal level, he was already alien to the

---

[19] Mikhail Lermontov, *Smert' poeta* (English translation: *Death of a Poet*, trans. John Woodsworth), https://ruverses.com/mikhail-lermontov/death-of-the-poet/8318/.

system of grandees, and on a cultural level he stood immeasurably above it. Hence the enmity towards it. (289)

Griboedov and others from the old Moscow families believed themselves to be the true nobles and inheritors of the ways of ancient Rus'. In their minds, they were the ones who correctly understood noble honor (*dvoryanskaya chest'*) and noble virtue (*dvoryanskoe dostoinstvo*). As A. Lebedev writes, these concepts were in direct conflict with service to the tsar (symbolized by the uniform— *mundir*):

> For ages the concept of noble honor and noble virtue had been in opposition to the *uniform*.[20] The tsar could deprive someone of noble virtue only through symbolic means of punishment. He could, however, dress someone in a uniform for full practical reasons. The uniform represented the tyranny of the tsar's power. The uniform was a sign of an *assignment*. The uniform superseded personality. People of Griboedov's and Pushkin's circle had a strained relationship "with the uniforms, with this pernicious hobby," wrote A. I. Herzen, "which was passed down from Peter III to Paul, from Paul to his children and to all the generals and commanding officers." This relationship existed for Pushkin the Kammerjunker and this relationship existed for Griboedov the minister (203).

For Aleksandr Herzen, writing later in the nineteenth century, honor was also more important than an allegiance to the tsar. In an especially venomous commentary on the post-Petrine era, Herzen singles out yet another population that stood in opposition to the old Moscow nobility—Russified Germans. A. Lebedev quotes his invective:

> Honor, of course, was more important than an oath to the tsar, for, according to the views of a nobleman such as A. I. Herzen, it seemed that for ages "the entire Petersburg establishment had been hanging by a thread. The throne had been occupied and

---

20 Chatsky mocks the *mundir* in his famous "А судьи кто?" (Who are the judges?) monologue as well, referring to those who only pursue rank and wealth: "Мундир! Один мундир! Он в прежнем их быту Когда-то укрывал, расшитый и красивый, Их слабодушие, рассудка нищету" ("The uniform is all! Right from the very start Their beautiful, embroidered uniform, a hollow Pretense, concealed their poverty of mind and heart," act 2, scene 4).

abandoned by depraved and drunk women, dullard princes who could barely speak Russian, children, and Germans. The closest road to Siberia and to hard labor lay through the court; gaggles of schemers and soldiers of fortune ruled the state." (202)

In the Russian text, Herzen's use of the feminine form of "Germans" refers to Catherine I and Catherine the Great, German princesses who married into the Russian royal family.[21] There were also many Russified Germans living on Russian soil, mostly in St. Petersburg. These Germans often held positions very close to the tsar and court life, especially during the reign of Anna Ioannovna, Peter's niece, in 1730–1740. In Griboedov's time, they seemed to be everywhere. By the middle of the nineteenth century, the German doctor essentially had become a commonplace in Russian literature. In his 2004 book *The Jewish Century*, Yuri Slezkine sees these Russified Germans as the most important "strangers" in Russian culture of Griboedov's time and beyond:

> Whereas much of Russian folklore recalled the battles against various steppe nomads (usually known as "Tatars"), the most important strangers of nineteenth-century high culture, were, by a large margin, German: not those residing in Germany and producing books, goods, and songs to be imitated and surpassed, but the internal foreigners who served Russia and the Russians as teachers, tailors, doctors, scholars, governors, and coffin makers. And so they were, mutatis mutandis, head to the Russian heart, mind to the Russian soul, consciousness to Russian spontaneity. They stood for calculation, efficiency, and discipline; cleanliness, fastidiousness, and sobriety; pushiness, tactlessness, and energy; sentimentality, love of family, and unmanliness (or absurdly exaggerated manliness). (113)

Griboedov did not hold Germans on Russian soil in high regard. Piksanov attributes this distaste in part to the time the author spent in Tiflis (present-day Tbilisi, Georgia) serving with General Aleksei Ermolov, a fellow member of the old Moscow nobility and a hero of the Napoleonic wars: "Ermolov most likely influenced Griboedov in one other aspect: Ermolov was a 'German-eater' and nationalist who had a hostile attitude towards foreigners in the Russian service" (267). Repetilov in *Woe from Wit* has a German father-in-law who refuses to

---

21 The irony is that Herzen himself was German on his mother's side (and a bastard).

reward his son-in-law with a cushy post—"Боялся, видишь, он упреку, за слабость будто бы к родне" (He feared a reproach, you see, for allegedly showing a soft spot for his family).

Significantly, Griboedov's first attempt at drama touched on a conflict between a group of Germans and a group of Russians. At Moscow University, from which Griboedov graduated at the age of fifteen, the Germans and Russians among the faculty apparently were often at odds with each other. The young author-to-be turned to drama to showcase his developing sense of humor, biting wit, and understanding of the social changes occurring around him. The result was an 1810 parody of V. Ozerov's 1807 historical drama *Dmitrii Donskoi*, with the humorous title *Dmitrii Dryanskoi* (*Dmitrii Worthless Sod*). The play poked fun at these warring factions of Russians and Germans. Judging by the subject matter of this early work, Griboedov at this time possessed at least a passing interest in social interactions that expanded to include the family unit in his next works of drama.

The very title of a subsequent play to which Griboedov contributed several scenes in the second act provides evidence that the writer was not only interested in how certain groups interact in society but was intrigued by the *svoj/chuzhoj* opposition itself as well. *All in the Family, or The Married Fiancée* (*Svoya sem'ya, ili Zamuzhnyaya nevesta*) premiered in January, 1818, written in collaboration with N. I. Khmelnitsky, a playwright who had enjoyed great success with his *The Chatterbox* (*Govorun*) in 1817, and the already accomplished dramatist Prince A. A. Shakhovskoi. The plot of the play, of which only excerpts remain, revolves around a young bride from St. Petersburg who tries to ingratiate herself with her husband's extended family in a town outside Moscow. She pretends to be someone else at first, arriving in town *pod chuzhim imenem*— under a stranger's/someone else's name.

Although *Woe from Wit* was not to be written for another six years, in *The Married Fiancée* we also see a character arriving from St. Petersburg into a situation where she may or may not fit in with a group of people whose ultimate judgment on her suitability is not to be taken lightly. There is a number of relatives whom Natasha, the young bride, must impress, and she uses different ruses with different people. Tellingly, however, the scenes that Griboedov contributed involve her interaction with an aunt who appreciates, above all else, family connections (*svoistvo*) and the Moscow way of life. In these scenes, we witness how Natasha brilliantly manages to weave her way into the good graces of this particularly difficult Mavra Savishna.

The newlywed's entry into the family is smoothed a great deal by another, more sympathetic, aunt, Varvara Savishna, who falsely introduces Natasha as the daughter of her husband's sister (*zolovka*), and thus, a relative of Mavra's in *svoistvo*. As Mavra reminisces fondly about Natasha's mother and father ("Your mother and I grew up together, the best of friends, and your father often came to our house in Moscow"), the reader (or viewer) of the play begins to get a sense of where this family comes from. Like Yankova, Vyazemsky, Shakhovskoi, and Griboedov himself, they are proud members of the older Moscow nobility. They are also impoverished (a circumstance to which Mavra alludes several times over the course of only a few pages) and look askance at the city of St. Petersburg and its inhabitants.

But the fact that Natasha has been introduced as a relation through marriage is not quite enough to win over Mavra. No, it is Natasha's relating of a caustic, gossipy tale of growing up in a prominent Petersburg home that eventually does the trick. Natasha shows herself remarkably adept at conversing with Mavra as a member of her clan would and should converse. She engages in the ostensibly harmless disparagement of friends and relatives that people who have known each other forever in this society inevitably enjoy (and which we will see in full bloom in *Woe from Wit*), she scorns wasteful spending (even sugar qualifies as a luxury), and, perhaps most importantly, she says the right things about St. Petersburg and the nouveaux riches to be found there.

> [...] Мне скоро щегольство
> И весь графинин быт: шум, пышность, мотовство
> И давка вечная в передней за долгами—
> Так опротивели, что рада, между нами,
> Была я убежать Бог ведает куда!
> Так опротивели! что лучше бы всегда
> Я ела черный хлеб, в серпянке бы ходила.
> Да лишь бы суетно так время не губила.

> [...] Soon the dandyism
> and the whole life of a countess: the racket, splendor, extravagance
> And the eternal throng in the foyer collecting debts
> Became so loathsome that, between you and me, I was glad
> To flee to God only knows where!
> So loathsome! That I would rather have eaten
> Black bread all along and worn flimsy linen.
> So long as I did not have to spend my time so vainly.

The stern Mavra Savishna is thus won over, and she herself suggests Natasha as an appropriate mate for her nephew Lyubim. Lyubim has fallen for a Petersburg woman who is not to the family's liking ("не по нутру") in part because Mavra and the other relatives believe that the woman is merely in it for the inheritance. Mavra's judgments on Petersburg are often contradictory; she disdains the nouveaux riches of the capital but then suspects them of trying to swindle her out of the money she has worked so hard to save from her three late husbands. Or perhaps Mavra is referring to family heirlooms rather than money, items (in Mavra's mind) over which a parvenu from St. Petersburg would presumably be salivating. For the older woman, it is important that Natasha is related to her by marriage and that, even though she was raised in a wealthy Petersburg household, she managed to retain the qualities that identify her as *svoya* (feminine singular of *svoj*).

As mentioned in Chapter 1, not all members of the old Moscow nobility stayed within their clan; many shifted allegiances to Peter in the early eighteenth century and lost the trust and confidence of their Moscow relatives. It is crucial for Mavra that Natasha did not stray from the true path (she actually uses the phrase: "с пути не сбилась"). In a later scene, Natasha's insistence that she is not some Petersburg profligate serves her well as Mavra begins to see through the young woman's dissembling and threatens to withdraw her approval of the marriage:

> ... И это все не ложь.
> По воле тетушки, кто я, от вас скрывала,
> Но в прочем ничего неправды не сказала.
> Хотя воспитана была в большом дому,
> Но цену знаю я, сударыня, всему

> ... And it all is not lies.
> According to my aunt's wishes, I concealed from you who I am,
> But otherwise I said nothing that is not true.
> Although I was brought up in an aristocratic house,
> I still know, madam, what everything is worth.

Although Griboedov may or may not have thought of some of the specific plot points for his later masterpiece while writing his contribution to *The Married Fiancée*, the notion that he was in many ways influenced by the elder Shakhovskoi, also a member of the old Moscow nobility (*svoi chelovek*), is certainly not far-fetched. Karlinsky makes the assertion that Griboedov was so influenced by Shakhovskoi's 1815 play *A Lesson for Coquettes, or The Lipetsk Spa* (*Urok koketkam, ili Lipetskie vody*) that any discussion of *Woe from Wit* that does not mention it would be remiss. It is not my project to prove Shakhovskoi's influence on Griboedov, but in any case, there are many plot points that *Woe from Wit* shares with *The Lipetsk Spa*. And it was Shakhovskoi who had earlier encouraged Griboedov to adapt a French play, *Le secret du ménage*, by Creuze de Lesser, for Russian audiences. Griboedov's 1815 *The Young Couple* (*Molodye suprugi*) was performed as a curtain-raiser at a benefit performance for a prominent Petersburg stage actress. Karlinsky sees the language in *The Young Couple* as inferior to Griboedov's contribution to *The Married Fiancée* and asserts convincingly that the author learned much from Shakhovskoi's *The Lipetsk Spa* and Khmelnitsky's *The Chatterbox*, both written in the interim between the two plays.

The title of another of Griboedov's dramatic collaborations, this one with Prince Vyazemsky, also questioned the current state of conventional familial relationships. *Which is the Brother and Which is the Sister?, or Deception after Deception* (*Kto brat, kto sestra?, ili Obman za obmanom*) was an 1823 *vaudeville en travesti* in which the main female character dons drag to teach her brother-in-law a lesson about prejudice. Although the play was a dismal failure, it shows us again how Griboedov was particularly interested in the subject of a subverted family unit.

Karlinsky writes that Griboedov began work on *Woe from Wit* only after he saw performances of *The Lipetsk Spa* and *The Chatterbox*. The first two acts were completed in the Caucasus in 1823. The author had begun and subsequently discarded a preliminary version of the play entitled *Gore umu* (*Woe to Wit*). In June of 1824, Griboedov, with the now completed play in hand, traveled to St. Petersburg to try his luck with the censors. He held readings for the likes of the writers I. A. Krylov, Khmelnitsky, Shakhovskoi, and the publishers N. I. Grech and F. V. Bulgarin, all of whom immediately responded to the play with enthusiasm. The censors, however, refused to deliver a prompt response to the work, much to Griboedov's frustration. Finally, in November 1824, Griboedov received word that parts of his play had been approved for publication in the January 1825 issue of the literary almanac *Russian Thalia*.

Griboedov's associates convinced the author to make more copies of *Woe from Wit*. His friend and fellow playwright A. A. Zhandr set in motion a copying process which produced an estimated 40,000 copies of the play by the 1830s, a phenomenon Laurence Kelly, in his book *Diplomacy and Murder in Tehran*, calls "a form of *samizdat* unequalled until Soviet times" (99). Bulgarin stated that he doubted there was a small town or literary household in all of Russia that did not possess a handwritten copy of the play. I will discuss the play's reception in more detail in chapter 3, but for now let me point out that as a result of the lack of movement on the part of the censors and this surreptitious and prolific copying process, *Woe from Wit* existed exclusively as a rough, handwritten text for *approximately seven years* before it was first performed on stage. In 1831, two years after Griboedov's death, the play was staged in excerpted form. There would be no full performance of the work until the 1860s.

As the copying and disseminating process was accelerating, Russia was in the midst of enormous social and political turmoil. Tsar Alexander I passed away on the first of December 1825, to be succeeded by his brother Nicholas I. Alexander's death was followed swiftly by the events of December 14, 1825, which would come to be known as the Decembrist Rebellion. Griboedov was certainly not unaffected by these events, and for some critics his political activism overshadowed his contributions as a playwright.[22] Although there are indeed elements of *Woe from Wit* that allow for a political reading, it is the social not political turmoil, that is more central to the essence of the play.

Western treatments of *Woe from Wit* seem to favor the commentary, either biographical (Kelly, Hobson) or linguistic (Costello), over a more sociological interpretation. Karlinsky effectively expounds on what he sees as misogyny and gerontophobia in the play, but does not really delve into the intricacies of the social scene of the day. Piksanov's 1929 article, however, is quite convincing on the merits of the social aspects over the political ones in *Woe from Wit*:

> Finally, the old criticism, with its tendency to discuss political rather than social problems, attached the wrong significance to certain major ideological elements in the play, the most major being Chatsky's attacks on the new service nobility. Historical evidence has established that these attacks link Chatsky with Griboedov himself, and with Pushkin, Ryleev, Vyazemsky, Lermontov—generally with an extensive network from the cultured, middling nobility. The antagonism to be found here is not political; it is the social antagonism of two heterogeneous groups of Russian nobles of the 20s and 30s. (295)

---

22 As Simon Karlinsky astutely points out, "Literature on Griboedov's possible involvement in the Decembrist conspiracy may well exceed in volume the literature devoted to the study of his great play" (284).

Another of these "social" scholars, T. I. Radomskaya, author of the 2004 article "Woe from Wit: The 'Strange' Comedy of a 'Strange' Writer" ("Gore ot uma: 'strannaya' komediya 'strannogo' sochinitelya"), perceives in the work a rift in the social fabric of the upper echelons of Moscow. For Radomskaya, this rift is embodied in the conflict between Famusov and Chatsky over a nobleman's duty in life: "What are the issues that cause the largest number of arguments between Chatsky and Famusov? Questions of morality, politics, serfdom? No. The most sensitive issue is that of a nobleman's duty and its fulfillment" (132). Radomskaya sees this conflict over a nobleman's duty as the manifestation of a clash between the old and the new in Russian society. "Old" and "new" are relative terms in this case, however. Although many people, including Pushkin as we shall see, saw Famusov as a representative of "old" Moscow, Radomskaya identifies him as a typical adherent of values passed down, not from generations of his Moscow ancestors, but from the newer nobility in the capital of St. Petersburg. By the same token, it is Chatsky, the dangerous "radical" who rejects what he perceives as servility and is later dubbed insane, who is represented as the true inheritor of the old Moscow families' understanding of a nobleman's duties. In this sense, then, it is Chatsky who is conducting his life according to the *svoj/chuzhoj* criteria laid out in Grandmother Yankova's memoirs. Famusov was born into the same world but is more in line with actions of the service nobility of the eighteenth century. After all, the ancient Moscow clans disdained what they perceived to be obsequiousness to the tsar and success measured solely by the acquisition of rank, attitudes they associated with the newer Petersburg nobility. In act 2, scene 2, Famusov praises his uncle Maksim Petrovich for his service to Catherine the Great, which included a willingness to make a fool of himself by falling down three times in a row in front of the empress at court:

> Упал вдругоряд—уж нарочно—
> А хохот пуще; он и в третий так же точно.
> А? как по-вашему? По-нашему, смышлен
> Упал он больно, встал здорово.
> За то бывало в вист кто чаще приглашен?

> And falls again. This time he planned it.
> More laughter, so he falls a third time. We'll be candid,
> What's your opinion? It's a chance we'd not have missed!
> The fall hurt but the rise was splendid.
> Who was more often called to take a hand at whist?

In the original, Famusov's wording directly invokes the opposition under discussion, in this case with *svoj* being replaced with *nash*: "А? как по-вашему? По-нашему, смышлен" (Well? What do *you* think? *We* think it was quite clever). Within his own story, then, Famusov allows, and is *prepared for,* two interpretations of his uncle's decision to play the fool in front of Catherine; in effect, he is already labeling the possible readings of the man's actions as *svoj* or *chuzhoj*. But who exactly are these two groups and who are their members? Their makeup is not clear after a mere cursory reading of the work.

With Famusov invoking the "old days" throughout the play, it is not surprising that the question of what was new and what was old confused even Pushkin, who, in "Moscow," the very same chapter from his *A Journey from Moscow to Petersburg* in which he waxed nostalgic about the harmless idiosyncrasies of the Moscow noble, bemoans the disappearance of Famusov from the city's social fabric: "*Woe from Wit* is already a ruined painting, a sad anachronism. In Moscow you will no longer find Famusov, who was 'glad to see anyone, you know'— Peter Ilyich, the Frenchman from Bordeaux, Zagoretsky, Skalozub, Chatsky, anyone . . ." (188). Pushkin goes on to list and lament the demise of the other minor characters from the ball scene as well. In his rush to praise the "good old days" of Griboedov's Moscow, Pushkin does not differentiate between Famusov and his ball guests, which, if one delves deeper, is a gross simplification of the matters at hand.

Radomskaya never uses the terms *svoj* or *chuzhoj* to assess the social situation in the play, but, in effect, this is what she is getting at. Moscow high society in the 1820s was approaching a state of significant instability. As the *raznochintsy* and the newer Petersburg nobility came to prominence, people no longer knew how to distinguish *svoj chelovek* from *chuzhoj chelovek*. In a play that consists mostly of people talking, the most important conversations depict the three protagonists—Sofya, Famusov, and Chatsky—as exceedingly preoccupied with identifying who is and who isn't *svoj*. Griboedov uses these characters' interactions to show the reader how difficult this once simple task had become at this specific juncture in Russian culture.

Whom exactly are these characters discussing, then? First, there is Molchalin, a classic *raznochinets*; he is most certainly not *svoj* by the old rules but seems to be making a strong case for becoming so. Then we have Skalozub, who *is svoj* but is actively rejecting the label. He is related to Famusov and Sofya, but seems uninterested in the connection. Skalozub values success based on rank and service to the tsar. Famusov, a member of the old Moscow clans, does not dismiss the importance of *svoi lyudi* but sees it as secondary to the acquisition of ranks through service.

Khlestova, Famusov's *svoyachenitsa* ("sister-in-law," "wife's sister")[23] seems to be a more traditional representative of the old Moscow nobility, but even she is beginning to change. And of course there is Chatsky, friend of the Famusov house, whose status as *svoj* would seem to be unshakable, but who is categorically rejected by the very people with whom he grew up. Sofya, for her part, must make a decision as to who—Molchalin, Skalozub, or Chatsky—qualifies as a suitable mate. And it is she who ultimately decides that Chatksy must go.

Let's take a look at the famous scene involving Famusov and Skalozub. Because of Skalozub's successful career in the military, Famusov sees the man as a perfect match for his daughter Sofya. Famusov becomes even more interested in the man upon hearing the news that he is distantly related to the family. When Famusov plays the *svoistvo* card with Skalozub, however, the latter responds with amusing indifference:

<u>Фамусов</u>

Ах! батюшка, сказать, чтоб не забыть:
Позвольте нам своими счесться,
Хоть дальними, наследства не делить;
Не знали вы, а я подавно,
Спасибо, научил двоюродный ваш брат,
Как вам доводится Настасья Николавна?

<u>Скалозуб</u>

Не знаю-с, виноват;
Мы с нею вместе не служили.

<u>Famusov</u>

Ah, my good chap, before I forget:
It seems that we are distantly related,
Although distantly, we won't share an inheritance;
You didn't know, I didn't either,

---

23 Khlestova is listed in the Cast of Characters as Famusov's *svoyachenitsa* (wife's sister). But Costello comments on Famusov's relationship to her: "Famusov introduces her to Skalozub as his *nevestka*, which, strictly, means his brother's wife. V. Filippov observes that this is in accordance with the old Muscovite custom of attributing to relatives, in their presence, a closer degree of relationship than they in fact possessed" (134).

I thank your cousin for the information,
How is Nastasya Nikolavna related to you?

Skalozub

I'm sorry, I don't know.
I did not serve with her.

Skalozub's incongruous response contains a very real sign of change in Russian society. Grandmother Yankova's far-reaching web of relatives and in-laws holds little significance for someone such as Skalozub. He is a man who respects the hierarchy of rank over the family connections to be found in the system of *svoistvo*. And perhaps in a concession to the reality of the times, Famusov, though seemingly perplexed by Skalozub's muted reaction to their shared relative, still regards him (a colonel after all) as the best suitor for his daughter. For many members of the old Moscow nobility, Skalozub's snub of *svoistvo* would have been a betrayal of his social background, another example of a member of the clan "going over" to Peter's side. Although such a "traitor" was then often shunned by the other members of their prominent Muscovite families, Famusov seems to ignore Skalozub's disinterest in their being distantly related. Skalozub and Famusov are on their way to this sort of betrayal in the name of fame and fortune (one possible origin for Famusov's last name is the Latin *famosus*—"well-known"). Famusov, at least, however, seems to want the rewards and fame without the work. The following excerpt is from act 2, scene 5.

Скалозуб

Не жалуюсь, не обходили
Однако за полком два года поводили

Фамусов

В погонь ли за полком?
Зато конечно в чем другом
За вами далеко тянуться

Skalozub

I'm not complaining. They didn't pass me over.
They kept me waiting for it for two years.

Famusov

All for a regiment?
Although it is in your nature—
The rest, I'm sure, lag far behind.

D. P. Costello comments on this exchange: "Famusov's thought appears to be that it is surprising that Skalozub should want a real command, with all the trouble that would entail, when, after all, the main thing was to achieve promotion and decorations as painlessly as possible" (165). Skalozub may be more like Famusov than he reveals. Critics have pointed out that Skalozub's medal may actually be fake. S. A. Fomichev writes in his commentary to the comedy: "No acts of war took place on the third of August—August 3, 1813—as a result of the Armistice of Pleiswitz, but a meeting did take place in Prague between Alexander I and Austrian Emperor Franz II at which they conferred a large number of medals" (671).

As for Molchalin, Pushkin's "good old days" would never have allowed a foothold in such an exalted place in society to Famusov's *raznochinets* secretary, the object of Sofya's affection and the pursuer of Liza, the saucy servant. Famusov makes sure to mention that Molchalin is the only employee of his who is not *svoj*: "При мне служащие чужие очень редки; Все больше сестрины, свояченицы детки; Один Молчалин мне не свой; И то затем что деловой" (It is very rare that a non-member of the clan works for me; they are all mostly my sister's and sister-in-law's kids; Only Molchalin is not one of us [*ne svoj*]; [I keep him] because he is such a good worker, act 2, scene 5).

However, because of Famusov's positive attitude towards service, Radomskaya sees him and Molchalin as more in step with one another than Famusov and Chatsky, who grew up in Famusov's house:

> Famusov, this "new" bureaucrat "of a new era," has a follower in the person of the young Molchalin. Lebedev has called the high-born Famusov an "apostate" specifically because of his views on service. And because of this he is close to Molchalin, he "of no kith or kin" (*bezrodnyi*), a man who lives not by the dictates of

family and ancestors (and in this sense "of no kith or kin"), but a man who fulfills first and foremost the demands of his "self." (138)

Lebedev also sees Famusov as a kind of traitor to his class: "But Famusov is an apostate. Famusov turned his back on the rules of the ancient families, on the nobles' understanding of independence. Famusov is a *servitor*, even though he does nothing. He is a servitor in his view of the world. He values people, like Skalozub, for example, by their rank" (205–206).

In fact, it is Molchalin, much more than Skalozub, who receives affection and attention from Famusov's ball guests. In act 3, the stern Khlestova actually calls Molchalin "родной" ("dear," but with the added connotation of blood relation and extreme fondness). In contrast, after Famusov introduces Skalozub to Khlestova, the grande dame complains to Sofya that her father is always introducing people to her without asking permission. And Khlestova is far from impressed with Skalozub's tales of military successes: "Не мастерица я полки-та различать" ("I am no expert at distinguishing the regiments," act 3, scene 12).

In essence, a closer look reveals that not all of the characters in the play are representatives of the old Moscow way of life depicted so lovingly by Grandmother Yankova and even by Pushkin. Of them all, Famusov is perhaps the worst example, with Skalozub and Molchalin following close behind. Famusov remembers the importance of *svoi lyudi* in the world of a Moscow noble, but sees them merely as a means to acquire material wealth and to control those around him. Into this new mix of social backgrounds and value systems steps Aleksandr Chatsky, who has been away from Moscow society for a number of years and has great difficulty recognizing it. Wherever he has been, either in St. Petersburg, in the West, or both, Chatsky's absence has not served him well in the Famusov household. In his 1895 article "An Insulted Genius" ("Oskorblennyi genii"), M. O. Men'shikov writes, on the subject of Chatsky's reception: "He is given the cold shoulder, as if he were a stranger/not 'one of them' (*kak chuzhogo*), as an outsider they had seen just the day before. Perhaps he had an outpouring of emotions in store—he is received as a mere visitor" (99). Even more importantly, Chatsky himself characterizes the household's hostility towards him in terms of the *svoj/chuzhoj* opposition: "С которых пор меня дичатся как чужого!" ("Since when do they shun me like someone not of their own/a stranger?," act 2, scene 4). Moreover, Famusov is so unsettled by Chatsky's return and so unsure of the man's status in his home that he does not even seem to know how to address him. Throughout the play, Famusov mixes the informal second person pronoun *ty* with the formal *Vy* when speaking to the man.

Many critics, in an attempt to explain why Chatsky receives such an unenthusiastic welcome from Famusov and Sofya, have pointed to the absurdity of a man arriving at a house like Famusov's unannounced, after such an extended absence, and so early in the morning. But to Chatsky, such behavior is entirely in keeping with the freedoms granted to *svoj chelovek*, which he assumes he still is upon arrival. There should be no ceremony on which he must stand; after all, he practically grew up in the house.

Much of the commentary on how the characters in the play perceive Chatsky as radical, transgressive, and alien ignores the fact that Chatsky and Famusov actually *agree* on many social and political issues, including those concerning foreigners on Russian soil and the role of women in society. Lebedev writes: "Within the antagonism between Famusov and Chatsky lies a desire on both their parts to figure out exactly where the two men stand in relation to each other. This task lies within the scope of a kind of class solidarity. They argue, but continue to remain 'in the same house.' It is only towards the end that Chatsky calls for his carriage" (206).

Similarly, Radomskaya comments (the book includes assignments for students who are studying the play):

> In his own way, Famusov is no dummy. Furthermore, several of his monologues, from the standpoint of their witty observations, could be attributed to Chatsky.
>
> **Assignment**. Read Famusov's monologue which begins "Taste, my friend, a haughty attitude" and write out the lines that Chatsky could very well have uttered. Compare Chatsky's and Famusov's attitudes towards foreigners and towards the role of women in society. (139)

As mentioned earlier, however, the two men certainly do *not* agree on whom exactly a Russian nobleman should serve. They clash almost immediately on this point, and it is in this part of act 2 that Chatsky utters his famous line, "Служить бы рад, прислуживаться тошно" (I'd be happy to serve, but being servile I can't stomach). The ensuing debate moves Famusov almost to hysterics as he labels Chatsky "dangerous," "arrogant," and "a revolutionary."[24] The middle-aged

---

[24] Famusov actually calls Chatsky a *carbonaro*, a reference to members of the Italian secret societies of the early nineteenth century that were instrumental in fomenting revolution in that country.

Famusov actually plugs his ears with his fingers like a child to keep out Chatsky's voice. But Lebedev sees the conflict as rather contrived:

> The two men actually understand each other perfectly. The discord in their dialogue is imaginary. Famusov doesn't not hear Chatsky; he *doesn't want* to hear what Chatsky is "preaching." And Famusov flies off the handle in his typical manner at the precise moment when Chatsky, in the midst of developing his thoughts on the grand differences between "service" and "servility," touches on his ideal: to serve "the cause, and not the faces." Famusov then simply announces that people with such ambitions must be sent into internal exile. (223)

Famusov wishes to forget his connection with his ancestors and confidently believes his value system to be the established "old" one of Russian society. Chatsky's "revolutionary" claims, upon closer look, are conservative ones. It is precisely because of Famusov's views on service and what it can do for him that Radomskaya interprets him as an inheritor of values taken from the "newer," that is, Petersburg, nobility (this despite the fact that he is clearly descended from the ancient Moscow gentry). Moreover, Radomskaya offers a decidedly different interpretation of another of Chatsky's famous phrases, "век нынешний и век минувший" (the present era and the era that has passed). She points out that the "era that has passed" for Chatsky is actually the eighteenth century, while "the present era" is a reference to ancient Russian traditions:

> Thus we see that there is a conflict reflected in the comedy *Woe from Wit*: a conflict between "old" ("ancient") and "new" traditions. This is not entirely what Chatsky is speaking about when he contrasts "the present era and the era that has passed." The morals of Catherine's court define Famusovian society, morals, which are, in relation to the centuries-old ancient Russian culture, new. It is these morals that Chatsky labels "the past era." "The present era" embodies Chatsky's views, but his service ideals are actually formed by the traditions of ancient Rus. In this sense Chatsky is expressing "the old ideas" concerning the purpose of a nobleman. (135)

Although this line of thought runs contrary to the conventional interpretation of Chatsky's role, it seems more convincing to look at the man's sudden presence as more of a reminder of forgotten roots than as radicalism incarnate. By the time Griboedov was writing in the 1820s, Peter's Table of Ranks had been in place for a full one hundred years and the age of Catherine was already enough of a bygone era to demand interpretation by writers who followed it. Griboedov, through his characters and their use of language, seems to be fully engaged in an assessment of the eighteenth century that was, according to Luba Golburt in her *The First Epoch*, relatively common for many people in the nineteenth century. On the one hand, the eighteenth century had faded enough into the past that it could be evaluated as old-fashioned, on the other, it was such a formative era for Russian society that it still was viewed, and rightly so, as modernizing. But the nineteenth century in Russia saw a fundamental change in how previous eras were interpreted, or, perhaps even more radical, in how successive historical eras related to each other and to the one following. Golburt quotes the philosopher Ivan Kireevsky writing about his contemporary 1830s: "defining the dominant direction of the age has become a common goal for all people" (7).

For Chatsky, then, the "dominant direction" seems to be movement backward; he is "defining his age," by emphasizing values and methods for human interaction that he ascribes to an era *before* the eighteenth century in Russia. But, as Golburt points out, nineteenth century modes of historicizing involved more than mere movement forward or backward or the marking of a monarch's reign; the century saw the assigning of styles, in the broadest meaning of the word, to historical eras. Style also includes language use, and language use and how it changes is a crucial element to a full understanding of *Woe from Wit*. Yes, Griboedov reflects the conflict between the generations in the play through the content of the characters' speeches, many of which touch on the subject of history, but also, most strikingly, through these characters' interpretation (both figuratively and literally) of the volatile *svoj/chuzhoj* opposition.

Golburt describes the effect this new way of interpreting history had on nineteenth century Russian society: "Quickly popularized, this conceptual shift required a striking array of adjustments, affecting intergenerational relationships within and beyond families..." (7). It is because of the specific manner in which Russian history developed and the particular relationship that the nineteenth century had with the eighteenth that the meaning of the phrase "the present era and the past era" is not as clear-cut as it seems.

For example, in Famusov's first lengthy monologue of the play, he is well on his way to shunting the old *svoi lyudi* to the side. Pushkin refers to this speech as evidence of the famous Moscow hospitality (*khleb-sol'*) but conveniently omits the parts where Famusov chides the providers of this hospitality: "А наши старички??—Как их возьмет задор, засудят об делах, что слово—приговор,— Ведь столбовые все, в ус никого не дуют, и об правительстве иной раз так толкуют, что если б кто подслушал их... беда!" ("And as for our old men, so passionate, what they say goes in their zest for judgment. They're all from the old families— they don't give a damn about anything.[25] The way they talk about the government, my heavens! If someone ever heard them, look out!," act 2, scene 4). Famusov is not only distancing himself from an older generation but is also removing himself from the ranks of the old families of which he is a member. He describes *them* as coming from the ranks of the ancient Moscow families (*stolbovye*) and not caring what others think of them, when in fact he descends from the very same stock. Famusov should be *svoj chelovek* in this crowd, but he does not want to be. A. Lebedev comments: "Famusov really is a living embodiment of the 'ladder of slavery' and servility about which Chatsky speaks so disdainfully and with such indignation. All of Famusov's words about a noble's valor, honor, etc., are just that—words. In reality, he couldn't care less about all of that. And that's why he has taken Molchalin into his home and drawn him close" (224). Famusov does not want to be reminded of the existence of an older system of determining who is *svoj/chuzhoj*, and the personification of this system is Aleksandr Chatsky.

Another point that many critics seem to have overlooked is that despite the cool reception Chatsky experiences from Sofya and Famusov, he actually is accepted *at first* as *svoj* by the guests at the ball. The first couple that Chatsky encounters, the newlyweds Natalia Dmitrievna and Platon Mikhailovich, receive him quite affectionately, certainly more warmly than Sofya or her father did. (Platon refers to Chatsky as either *brat* [brother] or *bratets* [dear brother] seven out of the ten times he speaks during their conversation.) Khlestova, with a gruffness that belies not a small measure of fondness, recalls that she used to pull Chatsky by the ears in his childhood—"только мало" (but not enough).

Moreover, Princess Tugoukhovsky clearly sees Chatsky as an eligible mate for one of her six unmarried daughters, at least until Natalia Dmitrievna informs her that he is not especially wealthy. One gets the impression that by the old rules, Chatsky's lack of an enormous fortune would still be a problem for the Tugoukhovsky clan, but one that could be overcome seeing that they are all *svoi*. Now things have begun to change, and for Famusov especially, the Chatsky's relative impoverishment is serious business and represents, at least at first, his best card to play to turn Sofya against the man (and against Molchalin for that matter). In the beginning of the play, Famusov tells Sofya: "Кто беден, тот тебе не пара" (A poor man is not a suitable match for you). Later, he tells Chatsky and

---

25 Mary Hobson translates this line as "These ancient families, they think themselves above us."

Skalozub, "Будь плохенький, да если наберется душ тысячки две родовых, тот и жених. Другой хоть прытче будь, надутый всяким чванством, пускай себе разумником слыви, а в семью не включат" (Let the man be a louse, but if he can come up with two thousand serfs, you've got your fiancé. The other guy could be sharper, puffed up with pride, who cares if he's known as a clever fellow, he'll never be taken in by a family). Considering that Famusov's expectations for serf possession is so high, the argument between him and his sister-in-law over exactly how many serfs Chatsky has is an amusing one. Famusov thinks he has 400, while Khlestova insists on 300. But for Khlestova, this 300 is a perfectly acceptable number for a member of the old families, while for Famusov, even the slightly higher 400 falls far short of respectability.[26]

If *Woe from Wit* were merely about a conflict between two differing interpretations of a Russian nobleman's duty in life, even taking into consideration the scintillating manner in which it was written, the work may have eventually disappeared into semi-oblivion like many of the dramas produced by Griboedov's contemporaries. The play's longevity in Russian culture is all the more surprising considering the at times harsh criticism that has appeared on the subject of its supposedly weak plot and numerous factual inconsistencies. Critics have long pointed out the seeming randomness of the scene order, the contradictions in the stances of the main characters, and a kind of over arching arbitrariness at play. (Remember that one of the assignments from the Radomskaya book asks students to find all the lines spoken by Famusov that could also have been placed in Chatsky's mouth.) Even as ardent an admirer of the work as Aleksandr Blok referred to the play as "случайна" (accidental). The literary critic Vissarion Belinsky, in an 1839 article on the play, also pointed out that many of the characters in the work often speak "out of character," or in the words of other characters. Lebedev quotes Belinsky:

> Belinsky noticed this oddity in the work in his article on *Woe from Wit* written in 1839 (more on it below): Griboedov has Chatsky speak at times "in the words of Famusov," and "Skalozub's barbs can really cut to the quick! Exactly like Chatsky, and, in a conversation with Molchalin, even Liza demonstrates a sharp tongue, uttering "a gibe that would do justice to the wit of Chatsky himself." (168)

---

26 It was not unusual for the "newer" service nobility to receive gifts of land and thousands of serfs from the crown.

A contemporary of Griboedov wrote, "The scenes are connected arbitrarily," to which the author responded, in a letter to P. A. Katenin, with whom he had earlier collaborated on the play *The Student*, "just as in nature, events occur in random order, whether small or important. The more unexpectedly they follow each other the more they arouse curiosity. I write for those who feel like me, and when in the first scene I can guess what will happen in the tenth, I begin to yawn and leave the theatre" (103).

There is more to the work, however, something about it that secured it a place in the canon of Russian literature. Despite the fact that, as mentioned before, very little *happens* in the play, there is one event that is quite significant. That event is Sofya's faux diagnosis of Chatsky as insane, a diagnosis that is made hesitantly, unstably, and, most importantly, using the term *ne svoj*.

After Chatsky witnesses Molchalin's servile behavior with Khlestova, he sarcastically praises him to Sofya, riling her to anger. Chatsky quickly exits. Soon after, Sofya is joined by "Господин Н." (Mister X), an unnamed party guest who offers a penny for her thoughts. Sofya replies that she is thinking about Chatsky, and when prodded to elaborate, offers the following: "Он не в своем уме," which, as a standard idiom in Russian, is usually translated into English as "He is not in his right mind/of sound mind" or "He is out of his mind." This rather strong statement regarding Chatsky's mental health does not seem to be fully understood, however, either by Sofya's interlocutor or by Sofya herself. Mister X asks her to clarify her statement, using a somewhat stronger Russian idiom to indicate insanity: "Ужли с ума сошёл?" (Is he really crazy?/Are you saying he's crazy?). There follows a significant hesitation on Sofya's part,[27] as if this interpretation of affairs is not entirely what she had in (sound) mind. She replies: "Не то, чтобы совсем…" (Well, not exactly…). Mister X prods further: "Однако есть приметы?" (But there are signs?). Sofya agrees with a reluctant "Мне кажется" (I guess so).

I reproduce the exact wording of the scene because most critics ignore it; they comment that Sofya calls Chatsky insane and that's that. But it seems clear that Sofya, even if she intended to plant this rumor from the very beginning, is actually startled by the phrase that comes out of her mouth. The actual wording of her "diagnosis," coming as it does in a play written at a time of instability for both the *svoj/chuzhoj* opposition and the Russian literary language itself, can be interpreted slightly differently. As I said earlier, it seems that neither speaker nor interlocutor in this scene really understands the statement "Он не в свое

---

27 The idea for the insanity diagnosis comes to Sofya in act 3, scene 1, when Chatsky mentions his unstable mental state. Sofya begins to think that she is the cause.

уме." Considering the title of the play, however, Griboedov was almost certainly careful in the line's construction.[28]

For help in formulating an alternative explanation of the statement, let us turn to a 1951 annotated edition of *Woe from Wit* published in England. In one of the many annotations printed in the back of the book (this one is numbered I. 4), the author, D. P. Costello, explains the expression, "Не спи" (Don't sleep), in Liza's opening soliloquy in act 1: "Imper. used in indef. sense: 'one must...' As often, *не* [the negative particle—J.G.] goes so closely with the following word that the resultant meaning is not negative, but positive. Not 'one must not sleep,' but 'one must stay awake.' Cf. such expressions as *не велеть*, 'to forbid'; *не стать* 'to cease'" (135). Along these same lines, when Sofya says to Chatsky, in act 2, "не свои беды для вас забавы" (misfortunes not your own are amusing to you), Costello's corresponding note is the following, "*не свои = чужие*. See n. on I. 4." (171). Costello is effectively telling us that through the rules of Russian negative commands and modifiers, the term *ne svoi* actually means *chuzhie*, an assertion that is in line, as I have mentioned, with many dictionary definitions of *chuzhoj* (explained as "*ne svoj*").

In light of Costello's linguistic explanation, the known instability of the language at the time, and the flux in which the *svoj/chuzhoj* opposition found itself, it is quite possible to interpret Sofya's initial comment not so much as a concrete diagnosis of insanity but as a rejection of Chatsky's former status as *svoj chelovek* in the Famusov household— "Он в чужом уме" (He is in a foreign/alien mind).

---

28 The word *um* in Russian has many meanings, including "mind," "intellect," and "wit." In Griboedov's play, however, the author seems to use it in at least one instance to mean "adventure" or "experience," or perhaps even "like-minded people." Sofya says, about Chatsky: "Ах, если кто кого любит, зачем ума искать и ездить так далеко?" (If someone loves someone else, why go so far in search of fellow travelers?). In this sense, the word is perhaps the antonym of *razum* (reason). The Russian expression *um za razum zakhodit* is used in common parlance to describe someone who is temporarily confused or crazed. But the phrase sets up the two components as representing two different modes of thinking: "Некоторые ученые связывают русское слово умъ с духовными способностями человека (ср. церковно-славянское прил. умный—"бестелесный, духовный"), а разумъ—с рациональным мышлением. Это выражение первоначально относили к людям, целиком полагавшимся на логическое мышление, в том числе к тем, кто пытался при помощи разума познать мир" ("Some scholars link the Russian word *um* [mind—J.G.] to a person's mental faculties [cf. Church-Slavonic adj. intelligent—"incorporeal, mental"], and the word *razum* [intellect, reason—J.G.] to rational thought. This expression originally applied to people who depended totally on a logical thought process, including those who sought to experience the world using their sense of reason," *Spravochnik po frazeologii*, https://www.rulit.me/books/spravochnik-po-frazeologii-read-140720-14.html). It seems Chatsky is more a representative of the word *um*, while others in the play represent *razum*.

This interpretation becomes even more potentially damaging if we consider an 1879 short story by Nikolai Leskov entitled "Driving Out the Demon" ("Chertogon"). In this powerful tale, the narrator witnesses the ritual of driving out the demon of *chuzheumie*— "foreign/alien/strange/otherwordly mind": "иже беса чужеумия испраздняет" (which casteth out the demon of foreign/alien/strange/otherwordly mind).[29] Tellingly, the narrator makes a point of stressing at both the beginning and the end of the story, which on a basic level revolves around the narrator being accepted as *svoj chelovek* and his attempt to get in touch with his roots in the people (*narod*), that the honor of witnessing the ritual can be had in Moscow and Moscow only: "Только сподобиться этого, повторяю, можно в одной Москве" (314). One can presume that this ritual would not work in St. Petersburg, the bastion of *chuzheymie* for the old Moscow clans. If we remember that Chatsky may have spent a considerable amount of time in the capital city, someone like Sofya, a Muscovite to the core, might have very well begun to diagnose him as possessed by this demon of "alien/foreign/strange/otherworldly mind."

Famusov, even before he hears the rumor of Chatsky's insanity, also seems to register the man's "difference." Significantly, in the first conversation that takes place between Famusov and Chatsky after the rumor has spread, Famusov uses wording similar to his daughter's original statement concerning Chatsky's mental health, again in the negative, and again a standard idiom, (this time a calque from the French):[30] "Любезнейший! ты не в своей тарелке!" ("My good man! You are not yourself/not in your plate!," act 3, scene 22). Two uses of the term *ne svoj* so close together may constitute a coincidence; three, to my mind, point to a deliberate calculation on the part of the author, and it is crucial that it is Chatsky himself who uses the expression *ne svoj* the third time.

Soon after Famusov's and Sofya's statements, it becomes clear that their words have begun to take their toll on Chatsky. He admits to Sofya: "Душа здесь у меня каким-то горем сжата, И многолюдстве я потерян, сам не свой. Нет! недоволен я Москвой" ("My soul is being squeezed here with some kind of sorrow, and I am not myself [one of my clan]. No! I am dissatisfied with Moscow," act 3, scene 22). Again, Chatsky's statement is a standard idiom in Russian meaning "out of sorts, dazed," but coming as it does third in a series of similar usages, the

---

29 Two translators of this short story into English completely ignore the *chuzhoj* root in the word *chuzheumie*. R. Norman translates it as "sinful thought," while Michael Shotton gives us "discontent."

30 The French word *assiette* means "situation," "base," and "plate." The expression that contained it was calqued into Russian either erroneously or jokingly using the word for "plate."

statement is more loaded than usual; thus it can be understood as "not one of the clan."

By having his characters use common idioms containing the phrase *ne svoj*, Griboedov may have been attempting to show his audience how volatile the term had become. It is perhaps fitting that the character who is first told about Chatsky's "insanity" has no real name; he is anyone and everyone in Russian (especially Moscow) society.[31] If Mister X does indeed represent Moscow high society as a whole, then his willingness to believe that Chatsky is insane represents the yearning of this society to possess a more recognizable definition to the once easily understood but now increasingly mystifying label of *chuzhoj*. It is not accidental, to my mind, that Mister X is uncertain as to the true meaning of the phrase, given that it was around this time in the history of the Russian literary language that the word *chuzhoj* was acquiring a different, more damaging meaning. V. V. Vinogradov writes in *The History of Words* (*Istoriya slov*):

> In the Russian literary language of the sixteenth to the eighteenth centuries, the word *chuzhdyi* belonged to the realm of the literary/written, while the word *chuzhoj* belonged to the vernacular, with no sharp differentiation in meaning. Naturally, the form *chuzhoj* was used almost exclusively in its basic meanings: 1) "not one's own, belonging to another or others" ("borrowed discourse," "to be called by someone else's name," "to live by someone's else's ways/by means of someone's else's thoughts," "to enter someone else's house," etc.); 2) "not related, extraneous" ("extraneous/unrelated people," "another's family"). It was much rarer to find the word *chuzhoj* in the meaning of "intrinsically distant in spirit," "spiritually alien" (cf. "You are alien to us," etc.). Thus, when the system of three styles collapsed at the end of the eighteenth and the beginning of the nineteenth centuries, *chuzhoj* and *chuzhdyi* began to be able to substitute for one another as forms of the same word, with, of course, certain stylistic connotations. (819)

I believe the play *Woe from Wit* both registered this development in the language and contributed to it. Once the diagnosis of insanity has been made and the rumor spread, the previously accepting guests react as if they had always

---

31 Originally, the labels for Mister X were written in the Latin script, implying perhaps that the man was French. Griboedov made a point of changing this to drive the point home that he was a typical Moscow resident, not a foreigner.

known about Chatsky's affliction. Famusov shrewdly brings up that insanity runs in Chatsky's family, a subject that to him now serves as a reason for the man's expulsion from society rather than as an idiosyncrasy that many Moscow noble families most likely shared. There was a time, one can imagine, not when one would not have believed such a rumor, but when the label "insane" would not have been so devastating. Pushkin pointed out in his reminiscences of Moscow past that people's idiosyncrasies were actually valued: "Невинные странности москвичей были признаком их независимости" ("The innocent oddities of Muscovites were a sign of their independence," 189).

Unfortunately for Chatsky, the time when these oddities were actually valued was already coming to an end. Famusov's power over Moscow society and his own interpretation of service had taken hold. In a way, his daughter's diagnosis of Chatsky as insane is a perfect example of Famusov's using someone who is *svoj chelovek* to advance his desires. Among all the inconsistencies in stances the various characters in the play take, there is tacit agreement between father and daughter that Chatsky must go.[32] But it seems that Chatsky irks Sofya for different reasons, something critics seem to have ignored.

Literary scholars, especially Soviet ones, tend to ignore Sofya almost completely in their zest to explain Chatsky's connection to the Decembrists and to the October Revolution. This tendency is curious, considering that Dmitri Mirsky writes, and I agree with him, that, "She is the principal *active* force in the play, and the plot is advanced mainly by her actions" (112). Gerald Janecek, in his article "A Defense of Sof'ja in *Woe from Wit*," cites the very same quote from Mirsky (as does Simon Karlinsky). For Janecek, the quote serves as an effective aid in his at times very astute characterization of Famusov's daughter. However, the author gets bogged down in an attempt to figure out whom exactly Sofya loves, a leap into the woman's psyche that the words in the text do not readily allow. What Janecek does identify correctly, to my mind, is the power Sofya has acquired in the years since Chatsky's departure: "In the intervening three years she has matured remarkably and is certainly his [Chatsky's—J.G.] equal, but she has also come to enjoy her position of power and superiority in the house" (321). Janecek goes on to point out that Sofya is clearly in the driver's seat in her

---

32 Although it is Sofya who makes the insanity diagnosis, it is possible that Famusov may have had a hand in it as well. Another possible etymology of the man's name is the Latin *fama*—"rumor." And at the end of the play, Famusov says the following to Sofya, in front of everyone, as if to convince them that Chatsky indeed is insane and he knew it all along: "Ну что? Не видишь ты, что он с ума сошел?" ("Well, see? Didn't I tell you he was insane?," act 4, scene 15).

affair with Molchalin; with this in mind Chatsky's abrupt return does not fit into her present plans.

For Janecek and his game of "she loves him, she loves him not," Chatsky's arrival constitutes a bad flashback for Sofya, who, now, as the powerful head of the household, does not want to be reminded that she once loved Chatsky and that he responded by fleeing to St. Petersburg or the West. But what Janecek misses is that what seems to bother Sofya the most about Chatsky is not the bad memories he forces her to confront but *the way he speaks*.

Throughout the play, we see Sofya complaining that Chatsky is rude, overly critical, and disparaging of Moscow society. Perhaps because of Chatsky's demeanor and the very title of the play, the critical debate over the years has revolved around who in the work is actually intelligent, to what degree a character is intelligent, and whether being quick-witted and mean constitutes being intelligent. Many, of course, see Chatsky as the misunderstood genius, expunged from society for his radical views. Others, including Pushkin, see Chatsky as decidedly unintelligent; a major indicator of an intelligent man, according to this line of thought, is the capacity to know to whom to display that intelligence, an ability that Chatsky clearly lacks.

Although I think the debate over who is intelligent in the play is as unimportant as the one over whom Sofya truly loves, at least Pushkin moved away from the content of Chatsky's monologues to the theme of social interaction, which is, in my view, one of the central topics of the work. Chatsky fails to interact correctly, most importantly, with Sofya. If we take a closer look at the form of Chatsky's speeches, we will see that Sofya is the only one troubled by his venomous *tone* (She calls him a "viper" early in the play). As mentioned before, the guests at Famusov's ball, at least until the rumor of insanity gets out, are quite accepting of Chatsky and his manner of interacting with them. After a few years away, which have sharpened his tongue considerably, he has returned to a milieu where a harsh comment has always been somewhat expected. As Chatsky's old friend Platon Mikhailovich says early on at the ball, "у нас ругают, Везде, а всюду принимают" ("We all say mean things, but are still received everywhere," act 3, scene 9).

It seems that Sofya, however, has grown to dislike this manner of conversing, especially when exhibited by someone her age. After Chatsky's first lengthy monologue upon his arrival, in which he takes gibes at all of the characters from their shared childhood, Sofya, instead of enjoying the memories or at least humoring him with a chuckle, suggests that he go sit with her elderly aunt: "Вот вас бы с тетушкою свесть, чтоб всех знакомых перечесть" ("I should put you in contact with my auntie to run through the list of all whom we know," act 1, scene 7). Sofya's reaction is decidedly *not* the annoyance of a girl who loves the people being mocked and yearns to leap to their defense. (One gets the feeling that she has heard the same kinds of comments from these people themselves.) No, she has merely grown tired of this type of discourse and associates it with her older relatives, perhaps the severe Mavra Savishna from *The Married Fiancée*, who, if we remember, appreciated Natasha's caustic comments and even interpreted them as evidence of her *svoj* status. Chatsky, in contrast, for all the experience he thinks he has gained while away from Moscow, still seems to speak like a member of the older Moscow clans. He has trouble understanding why Sofya does not laugh off his witticisms as mere words:

> Послушайте, ужли слова мои все колки?
> И клонятся к чьему-нибудь вреду?
> Но если так: ум с сердцем не в ладу.
> Я в чудаках иному чуду
> Раз посмеюсь, потом забуду:
> Велите ж мне в огонь: пойду, как на обед.

> Listen, are my words really so biting to you?
> And causing anyone harm?
> If so, then my wit and my heart are not at peace.
> When among odd birds I laugh once
> At another person's oddity and then forget it:
> Into the fire, if you want: I'll go as if to a dinner. (Act 1, scene 7)

Chatsky seems to be saying, "What's a little eccentricity among friends?" In this sense, his comments resemble Pushkin's fond reminiscences of the eccentricities of Moscow nobles. If everyone around him is *svoj chelovek*, and Chatsky, at first, seems to assume, perhaps naively, that they are, strange behavior (albeit of a certain kind) can easily be overlooked. Sofya, however, wants no part of this false camaraderie.

Later, in act 3, scene 1, Sofya again addresses Chatsky's tone: "Да! грозный взгляд, и резкий тон, И этих в вас особенностей бездна, А над собой куда не бесполезна" (Yes! A threatening look and sharp tone, And you have plenty of these traits, But you might benefit by looking in the mirror). Chatsky sees these qualities as normal; Sofya, especially after her time spent with Molchalin, is irked by them. By the same token, Chatsky cannot understand how Molchalin can remain silent while others abuse him ("Молчит, когда его бранят!"); it is precisely this character trait, coupled with an ability to soothe her father when he is excited, which pleases Sofya.

Whether or not Sofya truly loves Molchalin, the man is her recognized love interest of the moment, and it is his way of interacting with the representatives of the old families that Sofya holds up as an example for others to follow. Janecek writes, "Sofya's defense of Molchalin involves presenting him as a model of how Chatsky ought to act if he is to gain her sympathy. Molchalin is solicitous, mild-mannered, and taciturn, polite even to boring elders. She concludes that these features are better qualifications for family life than the traits Chatsky has displayed" (327). A. Lebedev concurs: "Chatsky is 'suitable,' perhaps, for 'feelings,' but clearly not suitable for marriage. Molchalin, it seems, is marriage material" (236).

Both Sofya and Chatsky notice the approval Molchalin's placid demeanor has elicited from the older guests at the ball. It is important to remember that at an earlier time in Russian history, Molchalin, a commoner, would not even have been allowed to approach a society woman like Khlestova. Sofya sees this acceptance as a win for her; Chatsky is bewildered and angered: "А он? . . . смолчит и голову повесит; Конечно смирен, все такие не резвы" ("And him? . . . he just hangs his head in silence; Of course he's humble, all of his type are," act 3, scene 1). Again we see how in the changing realm of social relations of the time, it is Chatsky who is actually the conservative one. He does not want to give the *raznochinets* Molchalin a chance, and does not understand how the man is making such social gains. The phrase "all of his type" is meant to be especially damning. Mary Hobson, in her 2005 commentary on the play *Alexander Griboedov's "Woe from Wit": A Commentary and Translation*, writes of the line: "The disdain is evident. Molchalin is not 'one of us'" (481). Although Sofya more than likely realizes that Molchalin is not "one of us," at least by the old rules, another reason she gives for why she appreciates the man is that Molchalin, unlike Chatsky, does not criticize people whom he (or others) sees as *chuzhie*: "Чужих вкривь и вкось не рубит" (act 3, scene 1). It is not clear who these people are for Sofya, perhaps the older generation, perhaps the Skalozubs of the world. This ambiguity is understandable given the instability surrounding this word at the time, but for Sofya it is more important, and more an indicator of fitting in, that Molchalin is respectful of everyone.

Therefore it is Chatsky, who, after refusing to change in his manner of social interaction, ends up excluded from the club. The joke is on him, literally. Sofya's "joke" (she says as an aside, as she sees the rumor begin to spread: "А, Чацкий! Любите вы всех в шуты рядить, Угодно ль на себе примерить?" ("Ah, Chatsky! You so love to make everyone else the butt of your jokes, can you handle the tables being turned?," act 3, scene 11), and the readiness with which Moscow society accepts it, show Chatsky as fully *chuzhoj*, fully expunged from the group, with no further say in who is *svoj* (one of us).³³

But why does Sofya reject Skalozub as well? Besides the fact that most any strong-willed young girl will almost certainly reject her father's choice for her future husband, Sofya may also believe that the stubborn Skalozub would not be as malleable as Molchalin, "he of no kith or kin." Like the instability that was present in the literary language of the time, Sofya's manner of communicating is not always classifiable (Pushkin commented, "Sofya is unclearly drawn"); at times she resembles a character from a sentimental novel from the late part of the previous century, or at least a caricature of one, as in the very beginning of act 1: "И свет, и грусть. Как быстры ночи!" ("With the light comes sadness. How quick the nights are!," act 1, scene 3). Sofya seems to think of her life in terms of some sort of novel, as evidenced by her famous comment regarding Skalozub from act 3, scene 1. When Chatsky calls the colonel a hero, Sofya retorts, "герой не моего романа" (a hero not of my novel), a double pun playing on the two meanings of the words *geroi*—"hero" and "protagonist," and *roman*—"novel" and "romance/affair." If Sofya is indeed writing the novel of her life, the largely unwritten Molchalin has more potential for her to develop. In contrast, for her, Skalozub, although perhaps a (military) hero, does not figure in her story.

As I stated earlier, many of the lines from *Woe from Wit* are quoted by Russians to this day, often without knowing the source. Chatsky's last words, "Карету мне, карету!" ("My carriage, my carriage!," act 4, scene 14), as famous as any others in the work, are employed by educated Russians in a social situation where they feel misunderstood, unwanted, scorned, or just plain bored. But where exactly is Chatsky headed at the end of the play? Many critics want to believe that Chatsky departs for parts more enlightened than reactionary Moscow; perhaps he goes abroad to start his own school or becomes a revolutionary. More likely he flees to his country estate and does what most old-guard *svoi lyudi* did for much of their lives: absolutely nothing. Laurence Kelly writes:

> Generations of critics have sought to analyse his [Chatsky's—J.G.] character. For Byelinsky, writing in the 1830s, Chatsky's protests against society were futile and quixotic; his precipitate flight from Moscow would lead to an "impotent exile, which

---

33 In the aforementioned argument between Famusov and Khlestova over how many serfs Chatsky possesses, which takes place after the insanity rumor has begun to spread, even Khlestova seems to begin to evaluate Chatsky as *chuzhoj*. She states, in support of her claim, that the number is three hundred: "Нет! триста! уж мне чужих имений не знать!" (No! Three hundred! Like I don't know other people's/strangers' estates!)

> in practice is a form of non-commitment, possible only for a *barin* [a member of the gentry] living off the the [sic] unearned income derived from his estates and serfs". In this, he agreed with Griboyedov's twentieth-century biographer Piksanov, who saw *Woe from Wit* as essentially a *barskaya* play, shot through with the values of the minor gentry: Chatsky, riding away in his carriage at the end, remained a landowner. (104)

Chatsky may have essentially taken his toys and gone home, this time to his imagined "real" ancestral estate deep in the heart of Russia.[34] Contrary to what has been written about his radicalism, he has refused to change with the times. This refusal to adapt to a new interpretation of the *svoj/chuzhoj* opposition, coming as it does in the midst of strong social and linguistic instability, has resulted in a confluence of the *chuzhoj* label with the diagnosis of "insane." From this time on in Russian culture, the word *chuzhoj* becomes, to varying degrees, a dangerous epithet, one used to slander rivals, to snub social inferiors, and to cut a loved one to the quick. The criteria for identifying who is *svoj* and who is *chuzhoj* will continue to change, but the damage caused by the *chuzhoj* label will remain severe.

A little later in the century the Russian reader is introduced to Pushkin's Tatiana Larina from *Eugene Onegin*. We are told that she is a morose, taciturn girl who spends her time sitting by the window rather than playing outside with her sister and her peers. Even within her family she is seen as different. But arguably the most effective method used by Pushkin to set her apart from her relatives and to convey this sense of estrangement is to label her *chuzhoj*. The following line is one of the first used in describing Tatiana and remains one that educated Russians can often quote by heart: "Она в семье своей родной, казалась девочкой чужой" ("She seemed a strange/foreign/alien little girl in her own family," 38).

In my next chapter I address the reception and distribution of *Woe from Wit* within the framework of the salon culture in which the work was discussed. I detail the play's enormous influence on a shift in how someone came to be accepted as *svoj chelovek* in the late 1820s and 1830s. It is during the time when *Woe from Wit* was being passed around to "those in the know" that we

---

34 Throughout the play, living in the country marks a person as odd, another change from the times when Moscow nobles spent a lifetime on their country estate. After the insanity diagnosis, Natalia Dmitrievna says, to support the claim, "А мужу моему совет дал жить в деревне" ("He advised my husband to go live in the country," act 3, scene 23).

begin to see Russians launch a sometimes frantic attempt to become or remain *svoj chelovek* and to avoid, almost at all costs, being perceived as *chuzhoj*. If, to paraphrase Simon Karlinsky, *Woe from Wit* is all about the words, acceptance into Russian salon culture of the time of its dissemination depended on knowing these words, and, more importantly, performing them.

Chapter Three

"Woe from Wit" as Social Gospel

Like his character Aleksandr Chatsky, Aleksandr Griboedov never found a social group in which he felt entirely comfortable. The author remained, for the most part, *chuzhoj* for the entirety of his short life. Critics have noted that the writer represented a transitional figure in Russian literary and social history, pointing out that Griboedov's masterpiece *Woe from Wit* contains elements of both the classicism of the eighteenth century and the Romanticism of the early nineteenth. Others have remarked that Griboedov himself to some degree belonged to several disparate social circles and literary associations but was not a solid member of any one group. Piksanov comments: "It is quite important to point out Griboedov's sociologically transitional position. It is characteristic (and unresolved) for Chatsky as well; we never do discover where he finds that little corner for his hurt feelings" (294).

Given this inability on the part of both the writer and his character to fit in and become *svoj*, it is all the more paradoxical that knowledge of *Woe from Wit* would become the mechanism for both the granting and denying of that status in the mid-to-late 1820s. Characteristically, it happened not only without Griboedov's help, but even against his will. Although Griboedov died in 1829, only five years after the dissemination of his play in manuscript had begun, he lived long enough to essentially lose control of his work and any influence over its interpretation. His readers had even taken to "correcting" the play in the copied manuscripts that they acquired, substituting what they thought were better rhymes. In *A. S. Griboedov—Woe from Wit*, Piksanov writes:

> The text became distorted not only because the manuscripts were unclear or the copyists ignorant. Fans also changed things, on purpose, at whim, daring to "correct" Griboedov. The copy that once belonged to Prof. O. F. Miller, and now belongs to Pushkin House, is characteristic in this respect: the text is so full of distorted words and phrases that one would think that someone made a concerted effort to rework Griboedov's text. (332)

Even worse, Griboedov saw the literary success of *Woe from Wit* eclipsed by its new status as society manual for livestock dealers (such as A. V. Kol'tsov), sons of serfs (such as M. P. Pogodin), and merchants across Russia to gain entry to the fashionable circles of St. Petersburg. As readers throughout Russia became *svoj* on the basis of a thorough knowledge of the play, Griboedov remained *chuzhoj*, often by his own choice, in all of the many social circles in which he traveled. These circles included the swiftly decaying realm of the old Moscow clans, made up of many of the author's childhood friends and relatives; the world of government service in St. Petersburg and abroad; and, finally, the newly professionalized literary sphere, with its representatives both in the capital and in Moscow.

A close look at the venues in which *Woe from Wit* was most often discussed, those of the literary salon and familiar circle, will show that these gatherings allowed a participant the opportunity to share his work with others and become *svoj*. The familiarity and closeness (*svoj*-ness) that the literary salons and familiar circles established between author and reader had real consequences for the narrative strategies adopted by later writers such as Aleksandr Pushkin.

One of the effects of these groups would be the Russian penchant for using proverbs and literary quotes in social settings. As mentioned earlier, to this day Griboedov's play remains one of the most quoted works of Russian literature. The years when *Woe from Wit* was being disseminated in Russia produced a keen interest in later generations for the use of these proverbs and literary quotes in a social situation, an interest that has not gone unnoticed by scholars and sociologists alike. Critics have pointed out that in social situations Russian culture still relies on and respects the proverb and quotation from literature more than other cultures. In *Russian Talk*, Nancy Ries writes:

> The use of conventional linguistic elements and clichés is not an automatic mark of banality. As George Gibian writes, "the Russian still trusts proverbs, and does not think he is being a parrot when he chooses to pick out of his memory a ready-made folk formula and applies it to a given situation". The central figure in a certain intellectual circle which I frequented was a respected scholar who always articulated a proverb, joke, or poetic couplet perfect for the moment or situation at hand. Such a skill (of memory and homology) is highly valued in most Russian discursive settings. A corresponding phenomenon is also greatly valued: collective delight often ensues when the occasion or the occurrence being discussed perfectly corresponds to the (pre-existing) cliché or proverb. This suggests a cultural appreciation of the integrity or continuity of social action/occurrence and discursive structures. (52–53)

My own experience in Russia attests to the claim that Russians appreciate "continuity in social action," through the use of proverbs and quotations, but I believe that it is their desire to feel *svoj* that prompted this appreciation. Many later Russian authors used lines from *Woe from Wit* in their novels and poetry, including Dostoevsky, whose provincial town residents in *Demons* quote Griboedov seemingly without knowing it. For Dostoevsky, it was not just the content of the play that was important, but how it was discussed in Russian society.

Griboedov's correspondence with his small group of friends shows a palpable unhappiness with his station in life. He consistently complains about all of the worlds with which he comes into contact. Although Griboedov was extremely respected in government circles, he claimed to serve only to feed his family. If this claim is to be believed, his attitude may have been noticed by others. According to a colleague, N. V. Shimanovski: "The men did not like him; he had an inconsistent personality and a self-esteem that knew no bounds" (*A. S. Griboedov in the Reminiscences of His Contemporaries* [*A. S. Griboedov v vospominaniyakh sovremennikov*], 121). Nor did the writer fit in with his Moscow relatives on their country estates, as he regarded them as lazy and corrupt. He sought approval in the literary world of St. Petersburg, only to lament how common everyone was. One commenter on the scene called him hard for many people to read (*nedostupen dlya vsekh*). As I mentioned earlier, he was on the periphery of the literary and political groups forming at the time, but never officially joined any of them.

Griboedov's impeccable pedigree, stretching back to the sixteenth century, only made things more complicated. His friends and relatives in the old Moscow clans, especially his mother, often criticized him for his desire to become a professional writer; they regarded this occupation as beneath the dignity of the scion of an aristocratic family. From Griboedov's letters, we can see that the author despised the views of his Moscow relatives and friends, which he found reactionary. *Woe from Wit* certainly had not pleased this constituency (the old *svoi lyudi*). Lawrence Kelly discusses the critic Vissarion Belinsky's comment on the reaction to the play in Moscow: "For the last few months of Griboyedov's stay in St. Petersburg, it [*Woe from Wit*—J.G.] was hotly debated in the literary journals. Belinsky recalled the storm of hatred it generated amongst the older generation, above all in Moscow. Griboyedov, who had once called Moscow 'my country, my family, my home', had betrayed his clan" (106). For his mother, this betrayal only intensified her disapproval of her son's desire to publish. In the following letter, the one from which Belinsky quoted, Griboedov complains to his friend S. N. Begichev:

> Moscow is not for me. It is the land of idleness and luxury with not the slightest link to anything good. People used to like music there, now nobody cares about it; there is no appreciation for the fine arts, and besides, "a prophet is not without honor, save in his own country, and in his own house." My country, my family, my home are all in Moscow. Everyone there remembers me as Sasha, a nice child who has now grown up, and after various youthful escapades is old enough to be fit for something, is appointed to a mission, in time perhaps can become a state councilor: beyond that they are not interested in me. At least in St. Petersburg there were some, let us say, who appreciated me more or less at my own valuation, and in the light in which I would like to be considered. In Moscow it is the very reverse. Ask Zhandr how contemptuously my mother once spoke over supper about my poetic endeavors. (Griboedov, *Complete Works* [*Polnoe sobranie sochinenii*], 3:133)

Here Griboedov describes how he has run up against the elitism and disdain often displayed by old Moscow families toward a member of their clan who has decided, not simply to write poetry and prose, but to make a living at it. For these people, writing was meant to be a hobby, not a career. In his 2002 book, *Natasha's Dance: A Cultural History of Russia*, Orlando Figes writes:

To be a nobleman was to take one's place in the service of the state, either as a civil servant or as an officer; and to leave that service, even to become a poet or an artist, was regarded as a fall from grace. "Service now in Russia is the same as life", wrote one official in the 1810s: "we leave our offices as if we are going to our graves." It was inconceivable for a nobleman to be an artist or a poet, except in his spare time after office work, or as a gentleman enthusiast on his estate. Even the great eighteenth-century poet Gavril Derzhavin combined his writing with a military career, followed by appointments as a senator and provincial governor, before ending up as Minister of Justice in 1802–3. (79)

If the old Moscow nobles had effectively lost the battle over whether one should serve the tsar, their ingrained snobbery had not disappeared. Instead, it shifted from a suspicion of the family backgrounds and intentions of Petersburg grandees and their attempts at ingratiating themselves with the tsar to an acute contempt for the professional writer. Griboedov's family fully expected the author to serve in a high-ranking position in the government and to dabble in poetry and prose at home. His mother, in particular, was adamant about this.

Griboedov and his mother never had an especially close relationship. Indeed, Natalya Griboedova gave her son scant maternal support throughout his life. She also seems to have felt that her son was not living the life that a Moscow noble should live. In addition, Natalya Griboedova was an enthusiastic supporter, à la Pavel Famusov, of career advancement above all else. Griboedov's sister, M. S. Durnovo, in conversation with D. S. Smirnov in 1826, spoke of her brother's relationship with their "Famusovian" mother: "Mother never understood Aleksandr's profound, focused personality and wanted only superficial glory for him" (*A. S. Griboedov in the Reminiscences of His Contemporaries*, 366). One of the only pieces of advice we know she offered her son was when he took up his first appointment in Persia. The advice, written about in a letter from P. A. Katenin to his friend N. I. Bakhtin (and republished in *A. S. Griboedov in the Reminiscences of His Contemporaries*), could easily have come from Famusov himself:

> Did I ever tell you that I by chance happened to read a letter about ten years ago that Griboedov's mother wrote to him? He had again entered the service with the rank of titular councilor and was headed to Persia with Mazarovich. His mother, delighted with the assignment, advised him not to follow his friend's, that

is, my example because supposedly I had gone nowhere by being honest and forthright. She suggested that it would be better to look to his relative for a role model, for he, as you know, although a scoundrel, is fast moving up in the world.

To Griboedov's mother, it was more important for her son to emulate the members of their family (the old *svoi lyudi*), regardless of what kind of a person that made him. This Famusovian view of the *svoj/chuzhoj* opposition, that one could and should get ahead in government service at all costs, preferably through family connections, is quite a bit different from the manner in which Grandmother Yankova described things as working in the Moscow she knew and for which Chatsky and Griboedov in many ways longed. In that time, the old Moscow families were fiercely independent (or so they thought) of the demands of the court in St. Petersburg, ignoring the upstarts around them who accumulated ranks and wealth to compensate for the lack of an ancient bloodline.

This "newer" interpretation of the *svoj/chuzhoj* opposition was apparently also shared by Griboedov's uncle, the man seen by many scholars as a prototype for Pavel Famusov. Griboedov writes in a piece devoted to his mother's brother and entitled *My Uncle's Disposition* (*Kharakter moego dyadi*):

> My uncle's disposition was one which has all but disappeared in our day, but which twenty years ago reigned supreme. I will leave it to historians to explain why a certain mixture of vices and politeness developed so pervasively in this generation; on the surface such chivalry in manners, on the inside such a lack of any kind of feeling... To explain this better, every man's soul harbored dishonesty and deceit. Nowadays this seems to have passed, perhaps not; but my uncle belongs to that era. He fought like a tiger against the Turks under Suvorov, and then prostrated himself at the feet of all those in favor in St. Petersburg. He lived on gossip in his retired years. An example of his moral compass: "*Me*, brother!" (Griboedov, *Complete Works*, 3:118)

This passage perfectly encapsulates the Famusovian worldview. Piksanov, referring to Griboedov's description of his uncle, writes in his notes to the 1969 edition of *Woe from Wit*: "One cannot help but notice that the very tone of this characterization strongly reminds one of Chatsky's monologues directed at Famusov" (370).

Despite the animosity between the writer and the old Moscow clans, Griboedov evidently still valued his family connections and childhood friends. However, he could hardly follow his uncle's example or his mother's advice on service and clearly was never able to truly immerse himself in the life of a government bureaucrat. As mentioned earlier, he claimed to serve in order to feed his family, and for no other reason. One feels the very real hurt in Griboedov's letters when he speaks about the disapproval his mother often doled out to her son. In one letter he expresses his pain to I. F. Paskevich in terms of the *svoj/chuzhoj* opposition. It is significant that immediately before Griboedov begins writing about his mother, he has been writing in French at length. He needs his native tongue, however, to express the true disappointment he felt after he read his mother's letter on the subject of his recent betrothal to the Georgian princess Nino Chavchavadze:

> Кому от чужих, а мне от своих, представьте себе, что я вместо поздравления получил от матушки самое язвительное письмо. Только пожалоста, неоценный благодетель, держите это про себя, и не доверяйте даже никому в вашем семействе. Мне нужно было *Вам* это сказать. (Griboedov, *Complete Works*, 3:240)

> Some people get it from strangers, but I get it from my own family. Can you believe, instead of congratulations my mother sent me the most venomous letter? Only please keep this to yourself, my inestimable benefactor. Don't trust even your family. I needed to tell *you* this.

Thanks in part to his mother's negativity, the author has all but completely lost faith in *svoi lyudi*, at least in the more traditional familial interpretation of the concept. If he cannot rely on his own mother for support, how can he trust more distant relatives? His plea to Paskevich, to whom he was indeed related, not to trust his own family with the information he has just relayed is the plea of a man who no longer feels *svoj* in his childhood environment.

St. Petersburg literary circles, it seemed, could offer new friendships and connections. As Griboedov mentioned in his letter to Begichev, people in the capital embraced the author on the grounds of his literary talent alone rather than on the basis of his family tree. The city's literati accepted Griboedov as a man of letters, and a professional one at that. But the author did not seem entirely comfortable either with this crowd or with the label of "professional writer," and it would be simplistic to say that Griboedov cut all ties with his Moscow clan in order to leap headfirst into Petersburg literary society. In some aspects, he remained a son of the old Moscow nobility until the day he died, and try as he might, could not always ignore the opinions of his friends and relatives. (Griboedov's sister's version of her brother's service in Persia has it that their mother had begged her son on her hands and knees until he finally agreed to take up the post.)

Although he no longer fit in with the hedonistic lifestyle of the Moscow estate-owner, Griboedov was not immune to his relatives' snobbery toward the profession of writer. This "divided personality" could, on the one hand, express outrage at his mother's opinions about his writing, but on the other, still harbor contempt for many of his fellow writers in St. Petersburg. Griboedov's Moscow noble upbringing clearly colored his opinions of some professional writers of the capital. Piksanov explains:

> Griboedov loved art and literature with a passion. He was alien, however, to professionalism, and here his noble upbringing came into play. While being interrogated on the subject of his role in the Decembrist uprising, Griboedov informed authorities that he had been a member of the Petersburg Society for Lovers of the Russian Word, but immediately added, "membership to which I excused myself for an extremely long time for I considered poetry to be the truest pleasure of my life, not my profession."
>
> Griboedov spoke of professional men of letters with more than a little noble condescension. In January 1825, he wrote to Begichev from Petersburg: "I had lunch yesterday with the dregs of the local literati. I can't complain; they were genuflecting and praising me to high heaven, but along with that I was fed up with their foolishness, gossip, tawdry talents and petty souls. Don't despair, my honorable friend, I haven't been completely wallowing in this quagmire of society." (293)

Piksanov's observations about the author's transitional personality seem remarkably astute: if Famusov in *Woe from Wit* represents a transitional figure in the sense that he, as a member of a class that once valued its clan above all and disdained government service, began to vigorously pursue rank and fame and viewed family connections merely as a way to get ahead, Griboedov in effect stood between his family, who thought like Famusov on the subject of government service, and the newly popular writer profession. From this angle, Griboedov and Chatsky have even more in common. Griboedov displayed many of Chatsky's character traits, including his sharp tongue, but, more importantly, a shared interest in the literary world (they were both translators and writers). In the play, Famusov compliments Chatsky on his writing and translation skills and once remarks on his eloquence: "и говорит как пишет" (and he speaks like he writes). If Chatsky does not flee to his country estate at the end of *Woe from Wit*, another possible destination for him might be St. Petersburg, where he could more effectively ignore his Moscow relatives and begin a new career by "re-specializing" as a professional writer.

Unfortunately, the accolades awaiting Griboedov and his play as the manuscripts made their way across Russia did not seem to give the writer much satisfaction. In fact, the author proved unable to escape his zealous fans. And then, a strange thing began to happen as these rough, hand-written copies of *Woe from Wit* began to pass from household to household in almost every city and provincial town in the country: people began to speak of the characters in the play as though they were *actually alive*. Laurence Kelly writes: "Even before extracts were published in the papers, those who had read the play in *samizdat* were talking of Famusov, Skalozoop, and Molchalin as though they were real people" (104). Kelly's choice of characters from the play's cast in the above quote is telling; it seems curious that Aleksandr Chatsky is not mentioned in this list— curious, that is, until we consider that the Russian reader, after reading of the man's expulsion from Moscow society, may not have been terribly eager to be associated with the *chuzhoj*/insane protagonist of the work.

As early as 1825, Aleksandr Griboedov and *Woe from Wit* were literally the talk of the town. I do not make a sharp distinction between the work and its creator because such a distinction is not possible. The play was linked in most people's minds with its author, the man who would read it aloud at intimate gatherings all over the two capitals. The distribution of *Woe from Wit* across Russia was so broad that Griboedov met a reader in almost every city and provincial town that he visited. As the author himself testifies, fans would often "perform" the work for him by quoting many of its lines and would speak to him about the characters as if they could be met in a drawing room any day now. As further evidence that Russian readers did not fully separate the author from his work, we have Griboedov's complaints in his letter to Begichev dated September 9, 1825, in which he relates how they drew conclusions about his personality based on the characters he had created. Griboedov bemoans the perils of being a popular author:

> And then there is the unendurable game of fate: all my life I have had the desire to find a small corner of solitude. For me it is nowhere to be found. I got to this place, didn't see anyone, didn't know anyone, and that's the way I like it. That lasted no more than one day. Either because of the reputation of my sister's piano-playing skills or someone sniffed out that I can play waltzes and quadrilles but these people came running up to me, showering me with greetings, and this little town quickly became more nauseating than Petersburg. But that's not all. Next came the tourists who know me from the journals as the creator of Famusov and Skalozub. So he must be a cheerful fellow. Confounded villainy! I am bored and disgusted! It is intolerable and joyless here! Although that's not entirely true. Sometimes they caress my ego overly much. They know my rhymes by heart and expect things from me that I may not have the power to provide. (Griboedov, *Complete Works*, 3:177)

Griboedov is evidently disturbed by his readers' belief that the creator of such wonderful characters as Famusov and Skalozub (note: again, not Chatsky) must naturally be a cheerful person. It is not clear to what Gribeoedov is referring when he confesses to being powerless to provide what readers demanded of him, but it could very well have been some kind of gesture that they could interpret as opening the door for them to becoming *svoj chelovek*. For what could be more reassuring to a Russian reader struggling to become *svoj* than a stamp of approval from the man who had shown them the importance of this status?

As Griboedov moved among posts in the Caucasus and the Near East and stays of varying lengths in both St. Petersburg and Moscow, apparently increasingly unhappy as the years passed, his play's popularity grew exponentially, especially in the realm of the literary salon and familiar circle. Although some scholars maintain that these literary salons and circles existed in Russia in the eighteenth century, the gatherings reached a high point in their popularity in the 1810s and 1820s. In fact, according to M. Aronson, Russian high society of the 1810s and 1820s in effect *was* the literary circles. He writes in his 1929 book *Literary Circles and Salons* (*Literaturnye kruzhki u salony*): "Within the conditions of Russian culture of the nineteenth century, literature played the dominant role" (20). Aronson comments later: "Russian society in the early nineteenth century was already heavily saturated with literature" (21).

These literary events had also begun to attract what some participants perceived as an increasingly motley crowd, as the social background of the members became more and more diverse. This diversity did not mean, however, that just anyone was admitted. If the eighteenth-century salon hosts composed their invitation lists by looking at their version of the *Social Register*, their counterparts a few decades later began to value different criteria—namely the *knowledge* of literature. As time passed, a close familiarity with literature, and the text of Griboedov's play in particular, replaced social standing as a means with which to secure an introduction to this social milieu. In his 1976 book *Fiction and Society in the Age of Pushkin*, William Mills Todd III writes, "Thus, a knowledge of literature and the ability to produce it—together with a measure of charm and some sort of introduction—became an entrée into social and governmental circles for ambitious young gentlemen without wealth or position" (62). Todd cites the reason for the increasing popularity of the literary salon as the collapse of the patronage system, which had reigned throughout the eighteenth century. Under the old system, a writer was under the "protection" of a monarch or high-ranking grandee. This writer would create works with his patron first and foremost in mind as his audience, and in exchange would receive financial and institutional support.

The patronage system had almost completely collapsed by the 1820s and 1830s, to be replaced by what Todd calls a "system of familiar associations." The familiar groups (*svoi lyudi*, perhaps, if translated into Russian) in effect leveled the playing field in the Russian world of letters, providing the writer with immediate feedback on his work and enabling the reader to participate directly in the creative process. A familiar group selected its membership ostensibly on the grounds of talent and knowledge rather than of bloodlines or wealth. There seems to have been no lack of success stories in which a writer of less than noble upbringing made a career of it in the once-hostile waters of literary high society:

> During the early decades of the century, the salons and circles included a number of literary figures of less than gentle birth. Zinaida Volkonskaia's Moscow salon (1824–1829) welcomed M. P. Pogodin, the son of a serf, and S.E. Raich, a priest's son, as did other Moscow literary groups, which fulfilled, on the whole, the salon ideal of openness to talent better than their Petersburg counterparts. N. A. Polevoi, scion of a merchant family, visited various groups of predominantly gentry membership and collaborated on a journal with Prince Viazemsky, subsequently a leader of the so-called aristocratic party of writers. Stankevich befriended a number of writers of humble origin, including the cattle dealer Kol' tsov. Nikitenko, later a professor and censor,

began his rise from serfdom by attracting the attention of influential circles. (62)

In fact, so many in Russian society were striving to move in the circles of the literary salon that at least one person began to question their motives. N. I. Gnedich, a poet and translator of *The Iliad*, had little time for the less serious participants in the familiar groups: "Our youth labors little for literature in particular and tries to fall in with litterateurs merely for some special ends and maybe out of having nothing else to do" (62). I would add to this statement that the youth of the time may also have been socializing in the familiar groups as much out of a sense of necessity as anything else. These evenings of literature and poetry had become the place where *svoi lyudi* could be found. Not to be up on the latest in the written word was to risk being labeled *chuzhoj*, an epithet that could end a career after Griboedov's play became so well known.

Gnedich is griping at a sort of frivolity and fun he perceived at these affairs, a complaint not surprising coming from a representative of the older generation known for his seriousness. From other reports, however, including P. A. Karatygin's account of Griboedov's encounter with the minor writer Vasily Fedorov, which I discuss later in this chapter, we will see that these evenings of literature could be quite contentious as well. Todd does not give us the sense of urgency, which propelled many people into these group, or of how uncomfortable they may have been at these affairs. After all, at the end of the day, no one wanted to become a Chatsky.

Although it can certainly be said that such a willingness on the part of the Russian reader to blur the line between fact and fiction when it comes to *Woe from Wit* serves as convincing evidence that Aleksandr Griboedov was truly gifted in depicting life-like Moscow society types of his day, it also points to the intense insecurity this reader felt. Thorough knowledge of the play's lines and a possible "friendship" with its characters in some way provided comfort to the reader in the time of social flux and instability both portrayed in the work and experienced by Russian society. The discussion and quoting of *Woe from Wit*, often in the context of the literary salons and circles of the 1820s and 1830s, became important criteria for determining who could become and/or remain *svoj chelovek*. In *Vek nyneshnii*, the Griboedov critic S. A. Fomichev wrote of the play:

> *Woe from Wit* had a special fate: it was to become one of the effective factors in the formation of Russian culture. The play became both an inexhaustible arsenal for those writing on social

affairs of the day and a school of craftsmanship for many Russian writers of the nineteenth century. It set in motion Russian aesthetic and social thought. (404)

But the play also set in motion social *interaction* as well. The success that greeted Griboedov's play was able to change the way in which Russians associated with one another at a time when society was experiencing extreme social and political turmoil. The transitional, unfinished, and unstaged state in which *Woe from Wit* existed would prove to be perfect for the venues that were gaining in popularity at the time as places to discuss literary works (among other things)—the salons and circles. In addition to providing an opportunity to critique and discuss a piece of literature, these intimate gatherings also allowed and encouraged an author (or reader) to transform a literary text into a performance in front of an appreciative audience. Despite the fact that by this time excerpts from Griboedov's work had indeed been published in journals, its status as an unfinished script for a play that had yet to be staged encouraged such performative acts. The pithy lines of verse and depictions of type, more than its plot, fueled its popularity and encouraged readers to quote it aloud.

In fact, *Woe from Wit* came to be regarded by some as a sort of religious text. More than one participant in the social scene of the day interpreted *Woe from Wit* as "social gospel," because of the guidelines it provided many a man with no ancient blood line of which to speak in his struggle to fit in Russian socio-literary circles. In a conversation with Griboedov's close friend A. A. Zhandr in 1858, D. A. Smirnov brought up the subject of *Woe from Wit* and its influence on Russian society:

> After a couple of asides, we struck up a direct discussion of *Woe from Wit*.
>
> "You know, Andrei Andreevich," I began, "I had made such use of it throughout my life, and earlier, as a young man, so often had used lines from it in my conversations, that one time a very clever woman said something to me that I will never forget: 'It seems that this is your gospel.'"
>
> "You think I'm surprised?" Zhandr answered. "Not at all. I want to surprise you with something in the very same vein. Did you know what was said, not to Griboedov himself, true, but to Bulgarin? This merchant, bearded, yes, but a man who loved to read, who in general loved enlightenment, said to him,

'After all, Faddei Venediktovich, this is our *society gospel* [*svetskoe evangelie*].' How do you like that?"

"What did he mean by that?"

"He meant that if in the real gospels we have rules for purely spiritual morality, then in *Woe from Wit* we have rules for society, for everyday morality ... (*A. S. Griboedov in the Reminiscences of His Contemporaries*, 235)

It is significant that it is a merchant who describes the play in these terms. This man was someone who had previously been unable to infiltrate the ranks of *svoi lyudi*. (Zhandr's condescending description of him as a bearded merchant who *nevertheless* enjoyed reading and enlightenment is telling.) Griboedov's play, and knowledge of its contents, had opened the door to him and to many others like him. The everyday morality of which the merchant spoke was being tested more and more in the context of the literary salons and circles.

As Smirnov's account proves, people began implementing lines from *Woe from Wit* in their daily speech as the manuscript was passed around. The most famous of these quotes, the so-called *krylatye slova*, or "winged words," took center stage. This same time period in Russian society also saw the publication of I. A. Krylov's fables, perhaps the only corpus of fiction besides Pushkin's that could possibly rival *Woe from Wit* in sheer number of lines that educated Russians know by heart and sprinkle into their conversation, often with no knowledge of their provenance. In *Vek nyneshnii*, Fomichev writes on the subject of these "winged words" in his article "'Woe from Wit' in the Context of Russian Culture's 'Golden Age'" ("'Gore ot uma' v perspektive 'zolotogo veka' russkoi kul'tury"):

> Suffice it to say that in Vladimir Dal' 's *Explanatory Dictionary of the Great Russian Language*, in which the author offers over 30,000 examples of proverbs, several dozen come from *Woe from Wit*. And keep in mind, Dal' was working from only his field notes. In this realm Griboedov can count only I. A. Krylov as a competitor. Krylov, however, left us over 200 fables; quotes from Griboedov that have entered the language come from only one work. (404)

Conventional wisdom has it that Griboedov's refreshing colloquial style and grasp of everyday life ensured the author's long-lasting popularity. While these qualities are certainly present in his works, the distribution of his writing also coincided with a sharp desire on the part of many Russian readers to fit in during the social chaos of the 1820s. In addition to being enjoyed for their aesthetic qualities, these lines became social tools to get ahead. By mid-century, these proverbs and sayings had reached a kind of exalted status in Russian culture.

In 1846, at the height of the Slavophile and Westernizer debate, Sergei Rimsky-Korsakov, son of Marya Ivanovna Rimskaya-Korsakova, from whose memoirs I quoted in chapter one, threw a masquerade ball that included performers who entered dressed in traditional Russian garb. They were led by a little person carrying a birch branch. Perhaps a greater effect was produced not by the little person himself, but by what was attached to the branch (from Gershenzon's *Griboedov's Moscow*): "A little person led them, carrying the beloved birch branch, from which hung multi-colored ribbons with traditional Russian sayings and proverbs written on them" (115). These quotes were used to such an extent that the line between literary quotation and proverb became blurred.

The play's popularity spilled over into the world of journalism, which could not have pleased Griboedov. As evidence of the ubiquitousness of *Woe from Wit* at the time, lines from the play made their way into all areas of the press, including advertisements in the newspaper *The Northern Bee* (*Severnaya pchela*):

> Quotes from *Woe from Wit* were used constantly in the same paper in editorials and feuilletons (including some quotes that had not yet been approved for publication)—sometimes with mercantile goals in mind—for example, "Famusov says in the comedy *Woe from Wit*:
>
>> The world is so well-made, you know!
>> You begin to philosophize—and your mind spins:
>> As soon as you settle, it's time for supper
>> You eat for three hours, and have three hours
>> Of indigestion!
>
> But where there is woe, there is comfort. The chic inhabitants of the Seine, the Athenians of the modern age, on the cutting edge in the world of the culinary arts, have come up with a number of remedies to alleviate Famusov's woe . . ." (there follows an advertisement for "alkaline digestive tablets"—*The Northern Bee*, February 26, 1827). (*A. S. Griboedov in the Reminiscences of His Contemporaries*, 397)

As we see from this advertisement, Griboedov was swiftly losing control of his work and its contents. Not only was the Russian reader now beginning to appreciate *Woe from Wit* as some do Shakespeare, for its abundance of pithy quotes, but they were now in a position to use these quotes to diagnose digestive difficulties. At times, Griboedov, perhaps realizing that his role in the play's reception was diminishing, would resort to pettiness. Bored with having to read his play over and over again, he would occasionally improvise at a literary gathering. In another letter to Begichev, Griboedov describes his approach to performing the text: "But when all is said and done I am so sick and tired of the same thing over and over again that in many passages I have improvised. Yes, this has happened several times. I then caught myself, but no one noticed. That's what's called bowing to the demands of the moment" (Griboedov, *Complete Works*, 3:156).

On at least one occasion, Griboedov even refused to engage in the fundamental activity on which the salons were founded—the sharing of one's work with others. Karatygin recalls that at a lunch reading arranged by one of Griboedov's collaborators on *The Married Fiancée*, N. I. Khmelnitsky, the writer Vasily Fedorov, whose play *Liza* had not enjoyed nearly the success of *Woe from Wit*, made the mistake of trying to compare the two works, however facetiously:

> While Griboedov was lighting his cigar, Fedorov came up to the table and picked up the manuscript, which was written in a rather sprawling style. Weighing it in his hand, he exclaimed with a naïve, good-natured smile, "Oh, how heavy it is—it's worth as much as my *Liza*!" Griboeydov looked at him from under his glasses and said through his teeth, "I am not a writer of vulgarity." (*A. S. Griboedov in the Reminiscences of His Contemporaries*, 108)

After Fedorov makes several failed attempts to apologize, Khmelnitsky tries to lighten the mood by telling Griboedov that the man will be put in the back row during the reading as a form of punishment. Griboedov, embarrassed not in the slightest at the severity of his reaction, will have none of the joking and calmly informs his host that under no circumstances will he read his play in the man's presence. Fedorov is forced to take his leave.

As well as illustrating the more than occasional moments of tension that occurred at these readings, this incident also reveals Griboedov's unwillingness to respond to any sort of criticism of his work in a constructive manner. Griboedov's refusal to share his work in front of an audience until the offender is removed, a rather twisted acknowledgment of the new system of *svoj/chuzhoj*, must have been truly devastating to a writer like Fedorov, whom most literary historians have described as "minor," a fate that may have befallen him at this very gathering. In any case, the man became close to persona non grata from that moment on.

Griboedov was just as hard on himself, however. The author's letters are replete with complaints about useless, gratuitous praise from people whom he did not respect. In September 1824, Griboedov actually ended a friendship with F. V. Bulgarin because of what Griboedov considered to be unwarranted and premature praise from the man. Griboedov lets Bulgarin down easy in this excerpt from the letter sent to him:

> I have to admit that I regret this because from the very first day we met you have shown me so much attention; the good opinion you have of me is, I believe, sincere. However, despite all this, I cannot continue our friendship. I do not have anything personal against you and know that your intentions were pure when you praised me under the name of Talantin. You did not intend to offend me. But my rules of decency and self-respect do not allow me to be the object of praise that is if not undeserved then at least overly premature. You praised me as an author, but I have yet to produce anything as an author that could be considered truly fine. (Griboedov, *Complete Works*, 3:161)

Still, Griboedov was not completely lacking in friends and confidants. In the following incident, the familiar groups seem to have been able to bring people together and provide the venue for the formation of lasting friendships. I refer to the case of Griboedov and Aleksandr Bestuzhev, another writer of the early nineteenth century. Bestuzhev, to be much better known in the 1830s under the pen-name Marlinsky, had steadily avoided Griboedov because of the latter's participation in a duel in November 1817. Bestuzhev had subsequently heard from Griboedov's enemies about the affair and had come away with a negative impression of the writer: "I was not well-disposed towards Aleksandr Sergeevich. His enemies' descriptions of the famous duel in which he served as a second cast him in an unfavorable light" (*A. S. Griboedov in the Reminiscences of His Contemporaries*, 97). This indifference evolved into a sincere interest in meeting the author of *Woe from Wit* after Bestuzhev devoured excerpts of the play, which Bulgarin had given him to read. But it wasn't until Griboedov read the play out loud that the friendship, in Bestuzhev's mind at least, was sealed. Griboedov invited him to a small gathering at a mutual friend's where he had planned to read from his play. From the moment Bestuzhev heard the final word read aloud, the two men were *svoi*:

> It goes without saying that I did not hesitate in accepting the invitation for the following day. The lunch was wonderfully fun, with no ceremony or rank involved. Of the half a dozen attendees, the group contained four men of letters. The reading began at around six. Griboedov was an excellent reader. He was able to give variety to each character and shade each successful expression without sounding false or turning the whole thing into a farce. I was in ecstasy. . . . After the reading was over everyone surrounded the author and showered him with congratulations and compliments, all of which he accepted very coldly. It was obvious that he had not decided to read the play in order to reap the rewards but rather to silence the incessant demands of the curious. I merely offered my hand, which he shook. From that moment on, we were no longer strangers to each other [*nechuzhdy drug drugu*] and I could be with him more often. (*A. S. Griboedov in the Reminiscences of His Contemporaries*, 102)

Bestuzhev's account points to some of the new criteria on which the *svoj* status has now come to depend. Griboedov's feelings about the evening are not to be found, however. Although it seems the author did indeed consider Bestuzhev a friend, it is far from certain that the author saw the reason for their coming together as linked to this particular evening.

By 1828, Griboedov had grown so tired of the obsequious fawning (and respect) from friends, critics, and fans over his play that he even began to doubt the worth of his masterpiece. One night, when praised for being so multi-talented, the author, an accomplished musician, diplomat, and linguist, demurred, saying: "He who has many talents lacks a genuine one." And in a letter to Begichev, he wrote, "Can I devote myself to something higher? How then, for what reason, can I say to people that their cheap approval and inconsequential fame in their circles can never give me comfort?" (Griboedov, *Complete Works*, 156).

By the time that Griboedov was preparing to depart for the post in Tehran that would prove to be his last, the fan base for *Woe from Wit* had grown too large and unwieldy; readers appreciated the play but not in the way Griboedov had intended. Most authors will be appreciated for qualities and reasons that they perhaps had not wanted to stress or had not even thought about. Not all authors, though, will scorn this praise and turn it against themselves. The author's self-assessment of his talents can be expanded to include the milieux in which he traveled: he had many but no real one. For Griboedov, perhaps the one real talent that he longed to possess was one not at all linked to literature, linguistics, music, or diplomacy: it was the ability to actually feel like *svoj chelovek*, something he never achieved.

Although Griboedov seemed not to want another diplomatic appointment and explained his reluctant acceptance of his final posting by stating that to refuse such an offer would have appeared to be the worst kind of ingratitude, the author may have actually needed to get away from the monster he had helped to create. Not only did he remove himself again and again to an entirely foreign world toward the end of his life, but he also chose to marry a Georgian woman rather than a Russian one.

There is little doubt that Griboedov's life and his masterpiece played a vital role in Russian culture of the 1820s. And at a time when the characters Griboedov created were often confused with actual people, real life meshing with a created world, it seems appropriate that reports of Griboedov's final days produced a scene more moving than many a fictional tale. When Griboedov departed Petersburg society in June 1828 to take on the position of Resident Minister Plenipotentiary to the Persian court, it was expected that he would return in a year or two as he usually did. But this was not to be. In January 1829, the author was massacred by a frenzied mob of Persians that attacked the Russian embassy. According to one account, Griboedov's body was so badly mutilated that he could be identified only by the scar on his pinky finger, which he had received in the duel with Yakubovich.[35]

In his work *Journey to Arzrum*, Aleksandr Pushkin describes a strange encounter, which may or may not have taken place, on the border between Armenia and Georgia as the poet was making his way to join his brother at the Turkish front. Pushkin encountered two men walking alongside an ox-drawn cart. When he inquired as to the contents of the cart, the men replied, "Griboed." The men were apparently accompanying Griboedov's corpse on its way to his young widow in Tiflis. This meeting has never been definitively proven or disproven, but it is true that Pushkin would later make a special pilgrimage to Griboedov's grave.

Four years later, in 1833, the first complete edition of *Eugene Onegin* would be published. Pushkin's narrator in *Eugene Onegin* is one of the first examples

---

35 Others have claimed his face was easily recognizable.

of the literary trend of "reaching out" to the reader that took hold in the 1830s. William Todd writes, "The earliest of these fictions, *Eugene Onegin*, is the one that does the most to project a familiar, conversational relationship with the reader, a relationship of the sort that characterized the salons and circles which still provided linguistic and literary codes for the incipient profession of the early 1830s" (92). Perhaps it is mere happenstance, but Griboedov's death did coincide roughly with a significant change in salon culture by the end of the 1820s. It was then that the salons ceased to be so egalitarian in make-up and the *raznochintsy* and others began to form their own groups. Todd writes: "The conduits that the literary groups provided to governmental careers and to literary repute were drying up by the late 1820s" (65).

According to Todd, Pushkin's chatty narrator in *Eugene Onegin* in part resulted from the absence of a real system of critics and criticism in Russia. But I would add that the choice to employ a homodiegetic narrator also stemmed from the desire to connect to the reader as authors once did in the salon. This type of narrator allowed the reader to feel *svoj* without attending an evening of literature. Yuri Lotman claims that the whole novel in verse was written in a kind of code for a select group of readers to decipher. This narrative strategy later took a solid hold in Russian literature, and we see it in various manifestations in Lermontov's *A Hero of Our Time*, Gogol's *Dead Souls*, and, most significantly for this project, later in the century in Dostoevsky's *Demons*. In that novel, as we shall see in chapter four, the homodiegetic narrator is so chummy and so desirous of seeming *svoj chelovek* to both the reader and to the residents of the provincial town where the story unfolds that his credibility comes close to being undermined.[36] Dostoevsky did not accidentally stumble upon this device; his choice to use him was part of a more general plan to direct the Russian reader's attention to the time period in Russian social history that he was most interested in critiquing—the 1820s.

As we will see, Dostoevsky was very interested in the fate of both Chatsky and Griboedov. Although he was to be fairly critical of both the character and the author, I will show that Dostoevsky eventually came to the conclusion that

---

36 At approximately this time, the so-called 'skaz' narrator gained popularity in Russian literature. According to Wolf Schmid ("Skaz," *Living Handbook of Narratology*, January 22, 2013, https://www.lhn.uni-hamburg.de/node/63.html), "*Skaz* (from Russian skazat' "to say, to tell") is a special type of narration cultivated particularly in Russian literature since 1830 (although, with certain differences, it can also be found in other Slavic as well in Western European and American literatures) whose roots date back to oral folklore traditions. It is characterized by a personal narrator, a simple man of the people with restricted intellectual horizons and linguistic competence, addressing listeners from his own social milieu in a markedly oral speech."

an interpretation of the *svoj/chuzhoj* opposition limited to the social plane was damaging Russia more than any one person or group; with this in mind, the fact that *Woe from Wit* had been interpreted as Social Gospel could not have pleased him. As we have seen, despite the fact that the criteria for becoming or remaining *svoj chelovek* in Russian society had changed numerous times since the institution of Peter the Great's reforms, with the label *chuzhoj* going from innocuous description to reputation-damaging insult, the sphere in which the two words interacted had remained firmly the social. It was this "oversight," if you will, that Dostoevsky sought to correct in his third major novel.

In order to redress this wrong, however, Dostoevsky was forced to make constant reference to the creative work in which the *svoj/chuzhoj* opposition's social component was most vividly depicted— Griboedov's *Woe from Wit*—as well as to the salon culture in which the work was discussed. Through at times subtle, at times obvious, manipulation of Russian readers' familiarity with Griboedov's play and the society in which the author lived, Dostoevsky hoped to alert them to other, woefully neglected, aspects of the interaction of these terms. A close reading of selections from *Demons* will examine Dostoevsky's interpretation of the opposition.

Chapter Four

The Demons are Social

Fyodor Dostoevsky wrote the bulk of his novel *Demons*, begun in 1869 and published in 1872, while travelling in Western Europe. It was not an easy time for the nearly penniless writer, whose fits of epilepsy became more severe during this period, and whose wife and daughter also suffered from poor health. In his notes for the novel, Dostoevsky describes an almost hallucinatory state that overtakes him at times, mentioning two especially disturbing dreams he experiences. Edward Wasiolek comments in the introduction to the translation of these notes: "Most of his fits come at three-week intervals, but at the time of writing they have increased in frequency. They come mostly at night, but not always without harm to himself from falls; the effects—headaches, heaviness of thought, and shattered nerves—last as many as five or six days. He cannot work, and the fits—either in Dostoevsky's imagination or in reality—are connected with other events" (3).

These events included the weather, the siege of Paris by the Prussians, and Dostoevsky's own personal struggles with the writing of his novel. But other factors may have also been troubling him. According to Nina Koroleva, the 1860s marked a new phase of interest for Dostoevsky in Griboedov's *Woe from Wit*. In her 1983 article "Dostoevsky and 'Woe from Wit'" ("Dostoevskii i 'Gore ot uma'"), Koroleva writes that the writer used character types from Griboedov to critique the social and political movements of the 1860s: "The

1860s represented a kind of new phase in the application of 'Woe from Wit.' The writer needed Griboedov's comedy as he had before. He quotes from it, choosing Famusov's words 'He reads, reads, and then— crash' as an epigraph to his article 'On Booklore and Literacy' from the cycle 'A Series of Articles on Russian Literature' in the journal *Time*" (119). Later in the same article, Koroleva writes:

> In the novel *The Insulted and the Injured* (1861) and in the journalistic piece "Winter Notes on Summer Impressions" (1861–1863), Dostoevsky uses Griboedov's types to characterize and evaluate the social movements of the 1860s. Dostoevsky compares the past and the present, transferring characters from *Woe from Wit* to his time, and referring to them as common nouns, as types. He now sees the need for both the main characters and the supporting cast, all the way down to Countess Khryumina, Khlestova, even Levon and Borenka, mentioned in Repetilov's monologue. (120)

Although Koroleva correctly identifies Dostoevsky's interest in Griboedov's masterpiece, she interprets the writer's appropriation of elements from the comedy as essentially stopping at the character level; I see a deeper connection between the two works. According to Dostoevsky's daughter, her father read *Woe from Wit* to his children frequently throughout their childhood; in fact, he read it so often that eventually he even yearned to play one of the characters on stage. For better or for worse, he never did, instead settling for more domestic settings to showcase his acting ability. Koroleva quotes the writer's daughter:

> Dostoevsky read and explained this comedy to us so often that eventually he was struck by the desire to play this role [of Repetilov—J.G.] himself, to show us how he interpreted it. He informed his friends of his intentions, and they suggested an amateur performance of the last act of the immortal comedy at their house. There was much talk about this interesting performance in Petersburg. My father wanted to face the public only when he was fully prepared, and he practiced only in front of his children. As always, he threw himself passionately into this new idea and took rehearsals very seriously, hopping up from the floor, after kind of falling at the entrance to the room, gesticulating and declaiming. (126)

Dostoevsky remained convinced throughout his lifetime that the actors he had seen perform the satire over the years had misunderstood both their roles and the play as a whole, and in his own interpretations at home he strove to correct the alleged errors he said he had witnessed.

In 1876, Dostoevsky wrote in his *Diary of a Writer* that he had by that point been reading and re-reading Griboedov's comedy for almost forty years. The author was not of one mind, however, about the contents of the drama over that long period; he changed his opinions and interpretations of both the work and its characters more than once. Dostoevsky admitted that he reached a true understanding of the character of Molchalin only after these forty years of familiarity with the play. The author's interest in *Woe from Wit* continued throughout the years when he was writing *Demons*, a novel rife with quotes and references to Griboedov's play and sharing with it many thematic points.

Although Dostoevsky remains one of the only major writers in the nineteenth century Russian prose literary canon not to have written a play for publication, the author was clearly interested in the genre. In fact, the novel *Demons* has more in common with the drama *Woe from Wit*, its author, and the culture surrounding its reception and dissemination than meets the eye. Let us first consider the form of the two works. In the chapter on Dostoevsky's novel in his book *Reading Dostoevsky*, Victor Terras writes, "The structure of *The Possessed* [an alternate translation of the title of the novel—J.G.] is scenic rather than narrative, in spite of pretending to be a chronicle. Dialogue and outright action dominate. Space and time are treated dramatically, as scenes are staged in symbolic space and time is arbitrarily adapted to the contingencies of dramatic action" (100).

Dostoevsky did not limit his borrowings from *Woe from Wit* to his novel *Demons* alone. He lifted quotes and themes from the comedy for many of his other works as well, including *The Insulted and the Injured* (*Unizhennye i oskorblennye*, 1861), *The Idiot* (1868), *The Adolescent* (*Podrostok*, 1875), and *The Brothers Karamazov* (1880). Dostoevsky paid particular attention to Griboedov's play, however, during the period he spent writing *Demons*. In fact, in rough drafts of the novel published by the writer's wife Anna Dostoevskaya in 1906, the character who would later become Ivan Pavlovich Shatov and who, critics have claimed, bears the closest resemblance to Dostoevsky in world outlook, performs an entire monologue on the subject of Aleksandr Chatsky and his worthiness. Although the monologue did not make the final cut, a significant number of other links to Griboedov's drama remained.

I have in mind a rather flexible definition of the word "link." On perhaps the most easily detectable level, there are the direct quotes and paraphrases from Griboedov's play found throughout the novel. More generally, there are the themes the two works share. And finally, keeping in mind that Dostoevsky was never entirely pleased with the performances of *Woe from Wit* that he had seen in his lifetime, it is possible that the author may have tried to stage a warped performance of the play within the framework of *Demons*. To that end, Dostoevsky even allows a version of the playwright himself to make a disguised appearance in his novel.

Much has been written about Russian writers and their tendency to quote their predecessors. Dostoevsky, no exception to this tendency, may have been up to something more than mere quoting, however. Alfred Bem, in his 1931 article "'Woe from Wit' in the Works of Dostoevsky" ("'Gore ot uma' v tvorchestve Dostoevskogo"), is quite convincing on the subject: "Analysis of Dostoevsky's oeuvre reveals that quotes from a certain work appear not only when the occasion is ripe or by mere mnemonic association, but almost always betray a certain ideological connection with the work being cited" (91). A thorough reading of the novel reveals that Dostoevsky was interested in far more than the mere plot of *Woe from Wit*; he was concerned above all with a kind of flawed, unnecessarily divisive interpretation of the *svoj/chuzhoj* opposition that he felt Griboedov's play and its reception in many ways encouraged.

As mentioned earlier, Dostoevsky made frequent use of Griboedov's work throughout the 1860s and 1870s. Considering this frequency, it would be difficult to ascribe the thematic similarities between the two works to mere coincidence. Alfred Bem expands on the subject of quoted lines in Dostoevsky to include the author's penchant for borrowing from other writers' *themes* as well. Bem does a little borrowing of his own to coin a term for this tendency, here from the field of music. He calls it *transponirovanie* (transposing), an artistic choice he considers not sufficiently investigated by critics and one that is crucial to the study of Dostoevsky's work:

> We can see how one episode from *Woe from Wit* came to the surface in Dostoevsky's consciousness in *The Insulted and Injured* and how distinctively he used it to achieve his artistic goals. For us this instance is interesting in the sense that it reveals a peculiarity in Dostoevsky's artistic style that has not been sufficiently noticed by researchers. I am speaking about the artistic device of transposing a certain thematic situation from another author and transporting it to different historical periods and to different social environs. The reshaping of another's material in cases like these is so great that it is very difficult to identify the original source. More often than not what marks

> the original source in such cases is a similarity in application of the artistic material on the level of ideas and semantics. I noted the most glaring example of such transposing in the scene in the elder's cell when Mitya Karamazov clashes with his father. The source comes from the famous scene in Pushkin's *The Covetous Knight* when Albert challenges his father to a duel. I am convinced that further research into the works of Dostoevsky from the standpoint of borrowed material will bring to light a great many more examples such as this one. (100)

Several instances of this "transposing" from *Woe from Wit* are present in *Demons*. The thematic situations that Dostoevsky chose to "transpose" from *Woe from Wit* to *Demons* are not accidental, and his referencing of Griboedov's play does not stop at the level of themes and quotations; it stretches to include a dialogue with Griboedov's interpretation of what it meant to be *svoj* and *chuzhoj*.

In her article on Dostoevsky and *Woe from Wit*, Nina Koroleva also sees the writer as being engaged in a dialogue or polemic with Griboedov: "Dostoevsky occasionally used Griboedov's works and ideas for his own purposes, other times he engaged him in a debate. The debate was sometimes a direct one, with references to specific characters from Griboedov's work. Other times the debate was more hidden, in the subtexts, but not difficult to recognize" (118). Although critics have been very adept at identifying the references to Griboedov's play in Dostoevsky's works, they have not been as effective in providing a convincing motive for them. To my mind, these references may have been employed by Dostoevsky more as moments of comfort for the reader, as landmarks on a path along a greater journey. As the novel develops and the references to Griboedov increase, on all the levels that I have mentioned, Dostoevsky is preparing to show the reader the havoc that the play has wrought on Russian culture. In his article "Fyodor Dostoevsky as Bearer of a Nationalistic Outlook," Louis Allain writes of the author's intentions in his major novels:

> The whole pathos of his large novels (for at the same time Dostoevsky was able to define in a significant manner the pathogenesis of some of the most serious contemporary illnesses, such as, for example, fascism and totalitarianism) stems from a fatal, yet, in its own way, logical displacement of planes. Not feeling under his feet sufficiently firm soil (and this from a *pochvennik!*), Dostoevsky the artist was forced, or, one should say, was condemned to endless proofs by rule of the contraries. (147)

Dostoevsky wanted to cure Russia of a certain self-diagnosed illness, and he strove to do this through a careful manipulation of how he understood the average Russian reader of the 1870s and that reader's specific frame of reference. In order to provide the cure for this illness, however, the author was forced to wallow for quite some time in the disease, a circumstance that could certainly have contributed to the struggles Dostoevsky experienced while writing the novel. Allain continues, "Dostoevsky as an artist-thinker was sometimes inclined to become dependent to a certain degree on the very thing he consciously damned" (148). The "consciously damned" component for Dostoevsky as it pertained to his novel *Demons*, then, is not the *svoj/chuzhoj* opposition itself but rather what the author considered to be the limited application of it that had taken a stranglehold on Russian culture, especially after the particular circumstances surrounding the reception of *Woe from Wit*.

To show the reader the consequences of this limited application of the opposition, Dostoevsky resorted to the depiction of a grisly murder, a tactic the author had employed before. According to Konstantin Mochulsky, it was not unusual for Dostoevsky to construct an entire novel for the sake of one scene: "While working on *The Idiot*, the author confessed that the whole novel had been written for the sake of the last scene (Nastasya Filippovna's murder)" (462). To my mind, *Demons* was also written for the sake of one scene— the murder of the nationalist Shatov.

This murder, coming as it does towards the end of the novel, amounts to far more than the elimination of one human being; it constitutes the elimination of a subtler and more ancient sphere of operation for the *svoj/chuzhoj* opposition, which, Dostoevsky believed, had been forgotten on Russian soil. Allain's "displacement of planes," as it applies to *Demons*, is a manifestation of Dostoevsky's attempt to urge the Russian reader to remember the other planes on which the *svoj/chuzhoj* once operated and, theoretically and ideally, could operate again.

The difficulty lay in revealing this to the Russian reader, of whom Dostoevsky expected a lot, in part because, as others have pointed out, the author himself was a careful and thorough reader. Alfred Bem goes so far as to call him a "reader of genius" ("гениальный читатель") in a 1931 article of the same name in which he reveals the links in Dostoevsky's *oeuvre* with the works of his predecessors, including Griboedov, Pushkin, and Gogol. Bem writes:

> Yes, Dostoevsky was a reader of genius. He had an extraordinary and artistic sensibility for other people's creative work. He did not merely read; he created along with the author he was reading

and really got into his characters, even placing them in different circumstances to force them to live a new life full of tumult and tragedy. The ideas discussed in the book he was reading excited him and he transformed them as well. From a mere hint or two, he managed to frame the deepest of problems on which he then expounded in his own work. He not only agreed with the author's stance but would often debate him, introducing his own understanding of the idea into the other's work, as if to show how he would deal with the issue if he were to choose a similar topic. (22)

There is no reason to believe that Dostoevsky did not expect the same perspicacity from his own readership. The author's references and allusions to Griboedov's play and the culture surrounding its reception are carefully placed throughout *Demons* to remind the reader of the issue that Dostoevsky was most interested in discussing, the *svoj/chuzhoj* opposition. Fully aware of how well most Russians knew Griboedov's work, Dostoevsky made sure that his novel was replete with familiar landmarks evoking *Woe from Wit*, all in an attempt to drive a point home and "save" the Russian reader from the narrow interpretation of the concepts that Russian society had adopted.

In her study, *Surprised by Shame*, Deborah Martinsen claims that Dostoevsky's writings are all about just that—"saving" the Russian reader:

> Like other Russian writers, Dostoevsky aggressively tries to mold his readers. While Karamzin aims to feminize his readers, Pushkin to remasculinize them, and Lev Tolstoy to estrange and educate them, Dostoevsky aims to save them. The most modern of Russia's nineteenth-century writers, Dostoevsky nonetheless embraces the unity of sociopolitical and metaphysical that characterizes the medieval worldview. (18)

It is exactly this unity that Dostoevsky was trying to return to the Russian reader; it remains to be seen if he succeeded. After all, in his 1880 Pushkin speech, Dostoevsky even coined a new term, *vsechelovek* (all-man) in his desire for Russians "to become the brother of all mankind" (*stat' bratom vsekh lyudei*). In his *A History of the Culture of St. Petersburg* (*Istoriya kul' tury Sankt-Peterburga*) Solomon Volkov writes: "Dostoevsky came to the conclusion that Pushkin's works contained a prophetic call for a 'universal unity'" (170).

Presumably, this unity could not be achieved with such a marked division between *svoj* and *chuzhoj*.

The story of Dostoevsky's rocky relationship with his mistress in the 1860s reveals a possible interest on the part of the author in the workings of the *svoj/chuzhoj* opposition (and provides more reasoning for his fragile state of mind while writing the novel). By the time Dostoevsky began work on *Demons* in 1869, he had engaged in a stormy romantic affair with the strong-willed Apollinaria Prokofievna (Polina) Suslova, who ended the relationship by rejecting the author's marriage proposal. Suslova, an author in her own right, would go on to write a thinly veiled autobiographical novella based on her tumultuous relationship with Dostoevsky. The title of this novella is significant: Чужая и своя (*Chuzhaya i svoj*; the English translation— *The Stranger and Her Lover*— ignores the interaction of the opposition completely).

Most scholars have been quite critical of both Suslova as a person and of her literary output. Edward Wasiolek, in his introduction to an English translation of *The Gambler* (which also includes translations of Suslova's diary and of some of Dostoevsky's letters), comments:

> The fictional Polina, Anna Pavlovna, is elevated into a purity and majesty that is far beyond realism and probability. Anna Pavlovna is the epitome of all virtues. Anxiety and suffering as well as "unconquerable strength and passion" are apparent in "her gentle and kind features." She is beautiful, complex, gentle, pensive, and trustful, chaste, modest, considerate, and on more than one occasion she is compared to the Madonna and the Christian martyrs. Losnitsky, on the other hand, the fictional surrogate of Dostoevsky, is petty, boastful, and vulgar; his only redeeming features consist in his appreciation of her majestic beauty, in his astonishment at having possessed her, and in his contrition at having lost her. (20)

Dostoevsky scholars have also pointed out that Suslova, who later married the writer and philosopher Vasily Rozanov, served as a prototype for many female characters in Dostoevsky's novels, including Nastasya Filippovna in *The Idiot* and Liza Tushina in *Demons*. The title of Suslova's work seems to have perplexed A. S. Dolinin, who wrote the introductory article to a 1928 collection that includes the novella, the diary, and several letters from her correspondence with Dostoevsky. He writes in a footnote: "The story *Chuzhaya i svoj*, with its fully established plot, was supposed to have undergone a number of changes on the levels of composition and style. We would have most likely seen the introduction of new motifs and new episodes that corresponded to the title, which, as it stands now, is not at all justified by the content of the story" (176). In fact, the title works just fine with the content of the story if we consider that the pair may have discussed the two poles of this opposition and their interaction in some detail when they were together. If we posit that Suslova knew that Dostoevsky was indeed trying to work out in his mind a less divisive interpretation of the *svoj/chuzhoj* opposition, she may have intended the title as yet another jab at her former lover, or at least as an attempt to reopen a dialogue on the subject with the author. Suslova's placement of herself first in the title (*chuzhaya*) is perhaps consistent with the selfishness that Wasiolek and others see in the woman, but she may have had something else in mind as well. The "alien/stranger" component, usually second, comes first; it is also in the feminine, making it stand out all the more. As Dostoevsky possibly tortured himself with the task of showing the Russian reader that these two words need not represent two mutually exclusive poles in a binary, Suslova may have wanted to say the exact opposite. The English translation of *svoj* as "her lover" in the title is wildly incorrect; it affords the Dostoevsky character in the novella more intimacy than Suslova envisioned. The title simply informs the reader that these two people are completely different and irreconcilably so; Losnitsky, the Dostoevsky character, is "one of us." He fits in, perhaps with everyone, in a way that Anna Pavlovna does not. With that in mind, any sexual relationship into which the couple entered was rather beside the point, at least for the purposes of the story. It is somewhat strange, then, that Wasiolek, when listing all of Anna Pavlovna's characteristics , does not mention perhaps the most pronounced one, the one from the title. Anna is "not one of us." If Suslova indeed intended to portray an exaggeratedly virtuous woman, proud of her attributes, it should be noted that she would be proud of being "not one of us" as well. It is this firmness of thought on the part of Suslova regarding the immutability of the opposition that would have perhaps irked Dostoevsky most of all. It also is noteworthy that Anna Pavlovna (most likely) commits suicide at the end of the novel by throwing herself into a river, a death that is somewhat similar to Shatov's in *Demons*, when he is thrown into a pond on the Skvoreshniki estate after being shot. But whereas Shatov (the unfortunate *chuzhoj* element in the story) struggles with all his strength to prevent his death, Anna Pavlovna ends her life on her own terms. It is as if Suslova is telling the reader, "Some people are outsiders and will always be so." Suslova's novella is not complex; she may have kept things deliberately simple if she wanted to drive home the point that this opposition is deeply embedded in the Russian language and culture and cannot be resolved or overcome. There can be no "salvation" from it. This line of thinking is exactly what Dostoevsky was fighting against in his novel.

Demons

The Setting

Among a stellar cast of murderers, adulterers, conspirators, and rapists in the novel *Demons*, the one character that elicits perhaps the most fear and hysteria is the one that is never named. It is the town itself, to which the narrator refers merely as "наш город" (our town) on the first page of the novel.[37] This appellation, both familiar and unfamiliar, sets the tone for the tale, with the narrator frequently referring to the locale as if everyone knows it and the members of its society, of whose makeup we never really get a sense.[38] The narrator often informs the reader of what "our town" and "our society" are discussing, how quickly everyone in the town found out about some piece of news, and how worried certain residents are that the town will find out more. Descriptions of someone's appearance or an event more often than not include phrases like "Весь город знал" (The whole town knew), "Все у нас об этом говорили" (Everyone in town was talking about it), or the oft-used "Город кричит/кричал" (The town is/was screaming about). Much like Famusov, whose famous exclamation at the end of *Woe from Wit*, "что станет говорить Княгиня Марья Алексевна!" (What will Princess Marya Aleksevna say!), typified that society's paranoia, each and every character seems to fear what the town will do if it "finds out" a certain piece of information.

But the two works share more than just the theme of paranoia running rampant in society. Although neither Chatsky nor Griboedov is referred to by name in *Demons*, many direct quotes and phrases from the play remain. As I mentioned earlier, the lengthiest interaction with *Woe from Wit* never made it into the novel; it can be found, however, in Dostoevsky's rough drafts. In a

---

[37] Or perhaps this naming without naming was deliberate on Dostoevsky's part. "Наш город" (or "н.г.") could be an inverted yet more specific reference to the personification of Moscow society who first spreads the rumor of Chatsky's insanity in *Woe from Wit*. Griboedov identified him only as "Г.Н." The town was possibly modeled on the provincial capital Tver, located at the confluence of the Volga and Tvertsa rivers. It is a major stop on the railway line between St. Petersburg and Moscow.

[38] The reader never finds out the narrator's full name either. We are told first that he is "Господин Г-в" (Mister G-v), a possible reference to the author of *Woe from Wit*. We later discover that his name and patronymic are Anton Lavrentevich.

discussion between Shaposhnikov and Granovsky (the prototypes for Shatov and Stepan Verkhovensky, respectively) in the drafts, the latter makes use of one of the many "winged words" from Griboedov's play:[39]

> *Granovsky* says: "To the pen from the card table, and to the card table from the pen. And there is a set time for high and low tide."
> *Shaposhnikov* immediately chimes in: "Chatsky, being the narrowminded fool that he is, doesn't even realize how very stupid he sounds saying this. He yells, 'a carriage for me a carriage!,' indignant because he is unable to see for himself that even in the Moscow of his time one could do better than 'to the pen from the card table, and to the card table from the pen.' He is a gentleman and a landowner, and nothing exists for him except his own little circle. That's why he becomes so despondent about life in the higher circles of Moscow, as if nothing existed in Russia beside that way of life. Like all Russian progressives, he overlooks the Russian people. And the more he overlooks them, the more progressive he is. The more one is a gentleman and a progressive, the more one hates—not conditions in Russia, but the Russian people. About the Russian people, its religion, its history, its customs, its destiny, and its huge numbers, he thinks only in terms of rent received. The Decembrists, and the poets, and professors, and liberals, and all the reformers until the time of the Emancipator-Tsar thought exactly in the same way. They collected rent, spent it living in Paris, attending Cousin's lectures, and ended up becoming Catholics, like Chaadaev or Gagarin. If they happened to be freethinkers, they would end up hating Russia after the fashion of Belinsky *e tutti quanti*. But what is worst of all, a Chatsky couldn't even imagine that there existed in Russia another world beside that of Moscow because he was himself a Moscow gentleman and landowner.[40]

While we of course do not know for sure why Dostoevsky chose not to include this monologue in the final draft of *Demons*, it is possible that the

---

39 Timofei Nikolaevich Granovsky, a history professor at Moscow University, is generally credited with the founding of the Westernizer movement in Russia.
40 *Vokrug Dostoevskogo*, ed. A. L. Bem, comp. and intro by M. Magidova (Moscow: Russkii put', 2007), vol. 1.

author's interpretation of the play may have moved from a desire to debate Aleksandr Chatsky's virtues and vices to a critique of how the Russian reader had incorporated Griboedov's work into his everyday life.

In addition, although Dostoevsky vacillated over the years in his evaluation of Chatsky as a person, he never could overcome a real sense of outrage over the man's estrangement at the hands of an unforgiving Moscow society, an outrage that explodes in the author's devastating description of the murder of Shatov, yet another unfortunate soul to be dubbed *chuzhoj*.

Another "winged word" from *Woe from Wit* can be found in a conversation between Liza Tushina and Nikolai Stavrogin (part 3, chapter 3):

> —По календарю еще час тому должно светать, а почти как ночь,—проговорила она с досадой.
>
> —Все врут календари,—заметил было он с любезною усмешкой, но, устыдившись, поспешил прибавить:—по календарю жить скучно, Лиза.
>
> И замолчал окончательно, досадуя на новую сказанную пошлость; Лиза криво улыбнулась.
>
> —Вы в таком грустном настроении, что даже слов со мной не находите.

> "The calendar says that it was supposed to be light out an hour ago, and it's still like night," she stated angrily.
>
> "All calendars do is lie," he was about to say with an amiable smirk, but, ashamed of himself, hastily added: "it's boring to live by the calendar, Liza."
>
> He fell silent for good, upset with himself over this new piece of vulgarity; Liza flashed a crooked smile.
>
> "You're in such a sad mood that you can't even find the right words when I'm around."[41] (467)

The above conversation serves as convincing proof that the average educated reader in 1870s Russia was so familiar with Griboedov's play (at least in Dostoevsky's mind) that at times this reader quoted from it not so much without thinking as *in place of* thinking.[42] Dostoevsky had found himself a powerful

---

41 Stavrogin was about to quote directly from the play. The line "все врут календари" (all calendars do is lie) is spoken by Khlestova in act 3, scene 21.

42 The exchange is not directly related to the discussion at hand. But, as Victor Terras points out in *Reading Dostoevsky*, such digressions only serve to heighten the dramatic qualities of the

teaching tool and he put it to effective use throughout the novel. Dostoevsky slows down the exchange; he does not have Stavrogin quote directly from *Woe from Wit*, he has the man *almost* quote from the work, making the line stand out even more.

For the generations that followed the dissemination of the play, Dostoevsky is reminding the reader, this type of interaction qualified the participants as "one of the clan." Dostoevsky questions this purely social interpretation of the *svoj/ chuzhoj* opposition here by having Stavrogin exhibit embarrassment at almost resorting to such a trite, memorized line from a play to express his feelings.

The Plot

One could say that the cowed, frightened atmosphere present in the novel's provincial town, its roots deep in the potential scorn from "society figures" expressed so vividly in Famusov's scream at the end of *Woe from Wit*, marks the most general link between *Demons* and Griboedov's comedy, and that the direct quotes mark the most specific. In between these two, we find themes shared by the two works. Both the play and the novel depict a society thrown into turmoil by the return of a man who had previously abandoned his home for the greener pastures of the West and/or St. Petersburg. Moreover, in both works this man is subsequently perceived as insane by the members of their unstable society.

One of the major differences, however, is that *Demons* increases the number of such portrayals by several orders of magnitude. In his zeal to make sure the reader has Griboedov's play firmly in his mind as he reads the novel, Dostoevsky seems to indulge in a bit of authorial excess. For if in *Woe from Wit* it is the return of *one* prodigal son from St. Petersburg and/or abroad to his hearth and home that throws all of Moscow society into a snit, in *Demons* it is the return of a score of Chatskys, almost a parody of that singular return, which contributes to the mounting hysteria in the provincial town. After all, it is not just Stavrogin who has recently arrived from abroad and/or the capital, but Varvara Petrovna, Stepan Trofimovich Verkhovensky, von Lembke and his secretary von Blum, Kirillov, Shatov, his sister Darya, his wife Marya, Petr Stepanovich Verkhovensky, Liza Tushina, Mavrikii Nikolaevich, Karamazinov, the Lebyadkins, and the entire Drozdov family as well. What's more, if we remember Chatsky's swift departure

---

novel: "The scenic quality of dramatic composition fosters improvisation in the form of casual digressions from the main line of action, such as inserted aphorisms, words of wit and wisdom, puns, and other word play" (86).

to parts unknown at the end of *Woe from Wit*, *Demons* depicts something of a mass exodus from the provincial town towards the end of the novel as well, as Stavrogin, Petr Stepanovich, Stepan Trofimovich, Lyamshin, and Liputin all take their leave, most of them to St. Petersburg. Stepan Trofimovich and Stavrogin subsequently exit this world entirely, following the Lebyadkins, Liza Tushina, the Shatovs, and Kirillov to their deaths.

And what about that insanity diagnosis from *Woe from Wit*? In *Demons*, it is certainly not Stavrogin alone who is thought to have lost his mind. At one point, Stepan Trofimovich tells Liputin that *he* (Liputin) has lost his mind when the latter brings up Stavrogin's possible mental illness. Later in the same chapter, the narrator informs Stepan Trofimovich that *Kirillov* may also be insane: "Stepan Trofimovich listened to my assurances distractedly, as if they did not concern him. I mentioned my conversation with Kirillov as well and added that Kirillov was perhaps insane" (115).

So what is Dostoevsky up to here? This thematic "overkill," if you will, may have been Dostoevsky's way to keep Griboedov and *Woe from Wit* in the mix to the utmost degree as the reader made his way through the novel, and not only, as we will see, via similarities in content.

The Audience and the Stage

As stated, *Demons* possesses qualities that link it more with a drama than with a novel. With Victor Terras's point in mind that *Demons* is often more scenic than narrative, I would like to consider a curious line that Liza Tushina utters in the heat of one of her monologues delivered in the middle of the street with Mavrikii Nikolaevich as her interlocutor. It is meant to draw attention to the performative nature of what is transpiring as they speak: "Lift your hat up a little, remove it completely for a moment, stretch your head towards me, stand up on your tiptoes. I am going to kiss you on the forehead now, like the last time when we parted. You see, that young lady at the window is fascinated by us ... Come closer, closer. Goodness, how grey he's gotten!" (101). Liza's acknowledgement of the audience viewing the spectacle that is unfolding both makes the scene more resemble a drama on the stage and again confirms the role of the town in this particular drama. The town in effect is the critic whose judgment the actors fear.

An even more theatrical (and bizarre) moment occurs later in the novel, in chapter 4 of part 2, as the narrator provides the back story for the new governor of the province, Andrei Antonovich von Lembke. In the middle of what has been a rather conventional narrative about the trials and tribulations of a government worker whose ancestry is German, the narrator informs us that after von Lembke failed in his attempt to woo the fifth daughter of a wealthy German general and distant relative, he decides to make a theater out of paper to console himself:

> Andrei Antonovich did not weep all that much, but instead glued together a theater made of paper. The curtains came up, the actors emerged, made gestures with their hands; the audience sat in their boxes, the orchestra mechanically moved their bows across their violins, the conductor waved his baton, and in the stalls the cavaliers and officers clapped their hands. It was all made of paper and all designed and constructed by von Lembke himself; he sat working on the theater for six months. The general purposely planned an intimate evening and the theater was brought out to be shown. All five of the general's daughters, including the newlywed Amalia, her factory owner, and many other young girls and women with their Germans, attentively examined and praised the theater; afterwards there was dancing. Lembke was very pleased and soon was placated. (284)

Von Lembke's coping mechanism for dealing with unrequited love is striking both for its originality and for the overwhelming approval with which it is met by the members of provincial society. It brings to mind the stories told by Dostoevsky's daughter of her father performing *Woe from Wit* at home for the family, but with an extra layer of artificiality added. Instead of a group of people performing at home in front of an audience, a group of people watches a person display a construct of people performing; it constitutes a double performance. Dostoevsky emphasizes Von Lembke's attention to detail over the course of the six months he spent on the construction of the theatre. The man is careful to follow all the conventions and rules associated with a night out at the theatre. Even though to most people a grown man spending six months on a paper theatre is perhaps more than merely idiosyncratic, by this society's standards he is acting appropriately in his grief and is rewarded for it by the town's praise and attention. At least for the moment, Dostoevsky seems to be showing, the rules of society are strong. Dostoevsky's wording of the line, "Андрей Антонович не очень плакал, а склеил из бумаги театр" (Andrei Antonovich did not cry too much, but instead made a theater out of paper), suggests that his decision was almost *expected*— as if this course of action would logically follow a moment of sadness.

The Opposition

The many references to performance and the more general shared plot points between Griboedov' play and *Demons* serve as purposely placed landmarks on Dostoevsky's literary map; their purpose is to elicit a certain reaction in the reader by the end of the novel. With the connection to Griboedov firmly ensconced in the reader's mind by the mid point of the story, Dostoevsky is able to pounce on the most crucial and devastating aspect of *Woe from Wit*— namely, the inability of an insecure society to determine who is *svoj* and who is *chuzhoj*— and then to expound on it exponentially.

In both *Woe from Wit* and *Demons* the family unit is depicted in a state of decay as sons and daughters quarrel with and/or deceive fathers, wives clash with husbands, and brothers argue with sisters. Writing on the subject of the provincial town's society in *Demons*, Edward Wasiolek perhaps puts it best in his introduction to the translation of *The Notebooks for "The Possessed"*:

> The first impression one gets of *The Possessed* is of incongruity, disharmony, and disfigurement. Everything is what it should not be. Intellectuals are not intellectuals, governors do not govern, and family relationships have unraveled: sons scoff at fathers, a niece finds the affection of an uncle an insult, and the respect a husband has for his wife increases when she takes a lover. Murder is considered fidelity; ugliness, beauty; blasphemy, religion; error, truth; and a million heads on the chopping block is the vision of the social millennium. (1)

Verkhovensky

One of the main causes of the paranoid atmosphere pervading the town is the appearance of Petr Verkhovensky, the leader of the "group of five," whose newer interpretation of the *svoj/chuzhoj* opposition only serves to add to the chaos. (We will see his ironic use of the term *svoi* later in a conversation with his father Stepan Verkhovensky). In chapter 6 of part 2, titled "Петр Степанович в хлопотах" ("Petr Stepanovich Bustles About"), Petr Stepanovich, in an attempt to ingratiate himself with the governor of the province, von Lembke, agrees to listen to the man as he reads aloud from his novel.[43] Although Petr is already in the good graces of Yuliya Mikhailovna, the wife of the governor, von Lembke does not share her positive opinion of the younger Verkhovensky. One day, Petr Stepanovich barges into von Lembke's office unannounced and completely without ceremony (not unlike Chatsky, at the beginning of *Woe from Wit*): "Петр Степанович взлетел в кабинет не доложившись, как добрый друг и свой человек, да и к тому же с поручением от Юлии Михайловны" ("Petr Stepanovich flew into the study unannounced, like an old friend and 'one of the clan,' and with an errand from Yuliya Mikhailvona to boot," 317). But the reasoning behind Petr's thinking he is *svoj* is decidedly different from Chatsky's. After von Lembke expresses outrage at the intrusion, Petr states: "And here I thought that if a man reads you his novel for two days running, in private, after midnight, and wants your opinion, then he's at least beyond these formalities" (318). Petr is relying on the interpretation of the opposition that emerged from the intimacy of the literary salons of Griboedov's time. Von Lembke, willingly or not, warms to this newer interpretation and understands what he must do. He winks at his relative von Blum, also present, as a signal for the man to make himself scarce, and with that, the blood line criteria for determining who is *svoj/chuzhoj* are removed. Von Blum is described as leaving with a long, sad face: "Тот исчез с вытянутым и грустным лицом" (319).

The anxiety over determining who is *svoj* and who is *chuzhoj* in a dysfunctional society manifests itself (in both works) in a stifling accumulation, relaying, and delaying of rumors and information. Almost every scene in *Demons* involves some mention of those gathered around to hear the discussion, debate over whether so-and-so who is in attendance is *svoj* (*nash*), and whether it is appropriate for the given subject to be broached in front of him. Although this tendency is understandably strong in the scenes involving the nihilists, it is in no way limited to their gatherings exclusively.

---

43 Andrei Antonovich von Lembke is not only the governor of the province; he also fancies himself a writer. In another nod to the salon culture of Griboedov's day, which encouraged people from all sorts of backgrounds to try their hand at the new writer profession, it is not only von Lembke (or Karamazinov) who writes in the novel. Gene M. Moore, in his 1985 article "The Voices of Legion: The Narrator of *The Possessed*," points out, referring to a piece of dialogue spoken by Varvara Petrovna: "To say that 'all of them write' is no exaggeration: Lembke is a novelist, Lebjadkin a romantic poet, Shigalov a ponderous graphomaniac, Liza wants to publish a book, Varvara Petrovna once tried to found a magazine, etc" (64).

A Stranger's Sins

To illustrate the difficulty in deciphering just who is *svoj* and who is not among the town's residents, let's take a closer look at one specific chapter in the novel, chapter 3 of part 1, significantly titled "Чужие грехи" ("Someone else's [a stranger's] sins"). Despite the multitude of characters in the chapter that makes use of the words *svoj*, *nash*, or *chuzhoj*, it is far from clear what exactly they mean by them. In several instances, the narrator speaks the words ironically (Dostoevsky has them italicized). In others, the characters themselves argue over who is *svoj* and who is not, or, when the characters can actually agree on a certain person's status, his actions betray it.

A pivotal scene in the chapter involves a conversation between the narrator, Stepan Trofimovich Verkhovensky, and Liputin, all supposedly *iz nashikh* (from our people), and a newcomer, an idiosyncratic man by the name of Aleksei Nilych Kirillov. In another allusion to Griboedov's play, the subject that occupies the men in this particular discussion is the mental health of Nikolai Stavrogin who has recently returned from St. Petersburg and the West. The first mention of the man's possible insanity produces a negative reaction in Stepan Trofimovich (note that the idiom Liputin uses to describe Stavrogin's mental state is similar to the one that Sofya uses in her first "diagnosis" of Chatsky in *Woe from Wit*):

> And then Stepan Trofimovich positively seized him: he grabbed him by the shoulders, turned him roughly around back into the room and sat him on a chair. Liputin even grew scared.
> "Well, what?" he began, looking carefully at Stepan Trofimovich from the chair.
> "I was summoned all of a sudden and asked 'confidentially' what my opinion was: Is Nikolai Vsevolodovich crazy or is he of sound mind ['в своем уме,' lit. 'in his own mind']? How is this not surprising?"
> "You've lost your mind!" Stepan Trofimovich muttered and suddenly lost control: "Liputin, you know quite well that you only came here for one reason: to relate some vile piece of news like this one and... something even worse!" (92)

What follows is Liputin's account of being called to Varvara Petrovna Stavrogina's house and asked to report on her son's state of mind when he and Liputin were in St. Petersburg. According to Liputin, Varvara Petrovna makes it clear that the conversation is to remain confidential. In return for Liputin's discretion in the matter, the wealthy Varvara Petrovna promises to help the man in any way possible. In this town of secrets and their dissemination, however, no conversation remains confidential. This one is no exception. Stepan Trofimovich attempts a half-hearted warning to Liputin not to divulge information to everyone in the room if it has been entrusted to him confidentially. Liputin responds hesitantly, revealing his own interpretation of what confidential means and who he thinks is *svoj*: "Совершенно конфиденциально! Да разрази меня Бог, если я... А коли здесь... так ведь что же-с? Разве мы чужие, взять даже хоть бы и Алексея Нилыча?" ("Completely confidentially! May God strike me down if I... and if here... but what, though? Are we really strangers [*chuzhie*], even Aleksei Nilych?," 94). Stepan Trofimovich's response to Liputin's invoking of the *svoj/chuzhoj* opposition is telling: "I am not of the same opinion; no doubt all three of us will keep the secret, but I fear you, the fourth one, and do not trust you with anything!" (95). This categorization of the group's members seems rather counter-intuitive. Up to this point in the story, the narrator has consistently referred to Liputin as *nash*. In addition, one would think that Kirillov, who has just met Stepan Trofimovich, should not be included in Stepan Trofimovich's *troe* (the three of us).

There are two other significant moments in the chapter involving the use of the term "one of us/one of the clan." Both involve Liputin. In the first instance, Stepan Trofimovich has to be reminded by Liputin who a certain Captain Lebyadkin is—"Тот самый и есть, **наш** Лебядкин, вот помните, у Виргинского?" ("That's who I am talking about, **our** Lebyadkin, from Virginsky's, remember?," 91). Later in the chapter, the narrator is grabbed by "our Lebyadkin" himself, who does not recognize him. Liputin reminds him: "— Это наш, наш!—завизжал подле голосок Липутина,— это господин Г-в, классического воспитания и в связях с самым высшим обществом молодой человек" ("'He's one of us, one of us!'—Liputin squealed from below, 'It's Mister G-v, a young man of classic upbringing with connections to the highest levels of society!," 110). It seems that the inhabitants of the town possess the *desire* to evaluate others through the *svoj/chuzhoj* opposition but their instincts (and memory, for that matter) are failing them. For Lebyadkin's memory to be jarred as to who the narrator is, Liputin is forced to praise the man in almost comically effusive language, which, significantly, points to Mister G-v's *society* connections.

The potential in the novel for any person in the town to be labeled *chuzhoj* is strong, and the following exchange between the narrator and Stepan Trofimovich illustrates the power of the word:

> "Stepan Trofimovich, are you really going back there? What good will come of it?"
>
> Stopping for a moment, he whispered to me as a pitiful, lost smile appeared on his face— a smile of shame combined with utter despair and a kind of strange ecstasy:
>
> "I can't marry a stranger's sins! ['Не могу же я жениться на чужих грехах!']"
>
> I had been waiting for this word. Finally, this sacred little word, hidden from me for so long, had been uttered after a long week of smirks and evasions. I positively lost control:
>
> "How could such a dirty, such a . . . base thought come to Stepan Trofimovich, to your lucid mind and kind heart . . . and even before Liputin!" (99)

The superficial explanation for the narrator's anger lies in Stepan Trofimovich's hinting that Darya is pregnant by another man. In this sense, Stepan does not wish to be the one to have to "cover up" this indiscretion by marrying the girl. The Russian idiom "жениться на чужих грехах" means precisely this—"to marry someone else's (a stranger's) sins." But the narrator seems to be irked more by the word *chuzhoj* than by the general sentiment. I maintain this interpretation for several reasons: the name of the chapter is *chuzhie grekhi*, the phrase *chuzhie grekhi* is in quotation marks when Stepan utters it, and the narrator refers to the word he has been waiting for as sacred (*zavetnoe*) hidden (*skryvaemoe*).

I am not the first to suggest that Dostoevsky's idioms can and should be interpreted on more than one semantic level. Olga Meerson's *Dostoevsky's Taboos* (1998) includes a lengthy chapter on *Demons*. In her discussion, Meerson addresses the metaphoric and literal meanings of those idioms that include the words *bes* (demon) and *chert* (devil) within the framework of taboo subjects present in the novel.

Similarly, in *Holy Foolishness: Dostoevsky's Novels & the Poetics of Cultural Critique* (1992), Harriet Murav argues for a literal interpretation of a different idiom involving the word *chert*:

> Stavrogin, in response to Gaganov's favorite expression that he cannot be led by the nose, literally takes Gaganov by the nose and leads him a few steps across the room. Later, on the pretext of revealing a secret, he bites the governor's ear. The narrator says that these schoolboy tricks were "unlike anything else" and were performed "the devil knows what for" (*chert znaet dlia chego*)

(PSS 10:38, D1.2). Precisely. The devil knows why Stavrogin played his pranks because they belong to his realm. (105)

Meerson uses Murav's observations and her own to argue that there is a strong precedent for interpreting Dostoevsky's idioms on the literal level, especially the ones containing the Russian words for "demon" and "devil." Although both critics make their case very well, I would submit that they overlook a perhaps not unrelated set of idioms: those involving the *svoj/chuzhoj* opposition. The narrator's extreme reaction to the word *chuzhoj* in Stepan Trofimovich's remark (with echoes of the terror Dolly Oblonsky experiences when faced with using the same word in *Anna Karenina*) could stem from his understanding of the word to indicate more than the simple "someone else's." Here it is not so much a matter of interpreting the idiom literally as it is interpreting it more "sinisterly" than intended, much in the same way that Mister X interpreted Sofya's initial diagnosis of Chatsky to mean that the man had lost his mind (*On ne v svoem ume*).

The fact that the phrase *chuzhie grekhi* is the name of the chapter and in quotation marks both times it is uttered certainly draws attention to it. In a way it is almost too obvious not to notice it. But if Dostoevsky is trying to point out to his readership the flaws in interpreting the *svoj/chuzhoj* opposition solely on the social level, he may have needed to be this obvious. The narrator interprets the word as overly negative, almost supernaturally so. If we remember Leskov's short story, "Chertogon" ("Driving Out the Demon"), which also links the word with the supernatural or demonic (*bes chuzheumiya*), we can see that the very demons and devils of which Meerson and Murav write so convincingly may also be present in idioms containing the word *chuzhoj*. And again, it is the narrator, a full participant (*nash*) in the goings-on in the town, who exhibits such a violent reaction to the "sacred" and "hidden" word.

If one of Dostoevsky's goals in this novel is to show that Russian reader need *not* interpret the *chuzhoj* element as sinisterly as the narrator and Stavrogin have interpreted it, he was forced to turn to the other term in the opposition, *svoj*, to show the reader how he had gone astray.

The First Argument

The opposition makes yet another appearance in *Demons* in the beginning of chapter 5 of part 1, "Премудрый змий" ("The Wise Serpent"), where an argument breaks out between old friends Praskovya Drozdova, mother of Liza Tushina, and Varvara Stavrogina. As in previous gatherings in the town, a special point is made at the outset to describe who exactly witnessed the events and whether those present should have been there in the first place. As the narrator sets the scene, he does his best to persuade the reader that the witnesses to this conversation most assuredly fit in with the participants and their presence should not cause anyone alarm: "I will add, finally, that the presence of those of us assembled in the drawing room could not have caused any special hindrance for these two childhood friends if a quarrel were to flare up between them. We were considered *svoi*, almost subordinate to them" (151). What seems a rather gratuitous remark on the part of the narrator becomes more significant if we consider that the town's residents are increasingly unsure of who is *svoj* among them.

When an argument does indeed flare up, Varvara Petrovna chastises Praskovya Ivanovna for revealing too much and tells her that she is lucky that everyone present is, indeed, *svoj*: "Varvara Petrovna sat up straight as an arrow about to be shot from its bow. She remained like this for about ten seconds, immobile, staring sternly at Praskovya Ivanovna. 'Well, you should thank God that everyone here is *svoi*,' she spoke at last, with ominous calm, 'You've said much that you shouldn't have'" (152). Praskovya understands Varvara's paranoia but pretends not to share it: "But I, my dear, do not fear society's opinion as much as some; it is you, under the pretense of pride, who quivers in the face of society's opinion. And the fact that we are all *svoi* here is so much the better for you than if *chuzhie* were to hear" (153). If the word *chuzhoj* is interpreted as truly sinister, Praskovya's use of it comes off as a potent threat. In any case, here the content of the argument is almost secondary to the commentary on who has heard it.

The Second Argument

A second argument more clearly presents the volatility that accompanies interpretations of just who is *svoj* in this town. In a startling exchange between Petr Stepanovich and Stepan Trofimovich Verkhovensky, father and son, later in the same chapter, the younger Verkhovensky states: "And here I thought that we were *svoi*, that is to say, your *svoi*, Stepan Trofimovich, your *svoi* and I'm actually *chuzhoj*, and I see that . . . I see that everyone knows something here and I somehow don't know anything" (186). Not insignificantly, this exchange takes place during a discussion of Stepan Trofimovich's pending marriage and of those pesky *chuzhie grekhi* (a stranger's sins) again. Later in the conversation, Petr Stepanovich returns to the term *svoi*, this time with the seeming intention of pointing out the worthlessness of the designation. In the midst of insulting his father, he offers up the compliment with heavy irony: "Forgive me my foolish confession, Stepan Trofimovich, but do please admit that even though you wrote to me you really were writing for posterity. It was all the same to you. Now, now, don't be offended. We are *svoi*, after all" (186). The semantic poles of the opposition are now completely breaking down. In a more normal situation, blood relatives, and certainly father and son, would have no reason to discuss whether they are *svoi* or not; it would be a given. And yes, this is not the first novel to address dysfunctional families and societies, but it is important to note the *way* Dostoevsky addresses them. He uses a tool specific to and readily understood by Russian culture, one that does not function effectively in translation into other languages.

The Duel

Petr Stepanovich's ironic usage of the term *svoi* shows how unstable the opposition has become. And yet the younger Verkhovensky is still clearly aware that it *can* be used in some way to make a point. But by chapter 3 of part 2, entitled "Поединок" ("The Duel"), we see how almost all the members of the provincial town have *forgotten* the possibilities afforded to them by the *svoj/chuzhoj* opposition. In the chapter, Nikolai Stavrogin and Artemii Pavlovich Gaganov meet to settle a score. There are several things that link this chapter and its resolution with Griboedov and his play, the first and most simplistic of which would be the somewhat similar names of Gaganov and Griboedov and the knowledge that Griboedov in his lifetime also participated in a duel. Furthermore, Dostoevsky apparently wanted to name a character in *Demons* Griboedov but changed his mind, perhaps so as not to be too obvious. In *The Notebooks for "The Possessed"* we find the following entry: "He marries the daughter of a minister of state. *The main thing.* Prior to the Prince's arrival, rumors are heard in town about his connections with the highest circles in Petersburg, with ministers [Griboedov]" (211).

The second link is the narrator's rather lengthy description of Gaganov's background, a description that could conceivably be applied to the author of *Woe from Wit*: "One more trait: he belonged to that strange but still extant brand of Russian nobleman who truly cherishes the antiquity and purity of his noble line and takes it rather too seriously" (262). On the subject of Gaganov's career, the narrator informs us: "This tense, extremely stern man, who knew his service duties and fulfilled his responsibilities extremely well, was in his heart a dreamer" (262). Griboedov, if we remember, was also a career diplomat who knew his service duties well, but who, in his soul, was a "dreamer" (a writer).

During the duel, Gaganov's first shot nicks Stavrogin's pinky finger, which is the spot where Griboedov was hit during his duel with Yakubovich: "Yakubovich came up to the *barriere*, with a bold step, and awaited Griboyedov's shot. Griboyedov took two steps. They stood motionless facing each other in this way for a minute, then Yakubovich lost patience and fired, aiming at the leg since he did not wish to kill Griboyedov. The bullet hit the little finger of Griboyedov's left hand, Yakubovich apparently exclaiming, 'At least he will have to stop playing the piano.'"[44] The resulting scar was by some accounts the only way that Griboedov's body could be identified after he was murdered and dragged through the streets of Tehran by a Persian mob.

For this project, however, the most pertinent piece of information linking this duel with Griboedov's play is the (delayed) appearance of the *svoj/chuzhoj* opposition in evaluating what has transpired. In the chapter that follows "The Duel," entitled "Все в ожидании" ("All in Expectation"), the narrator tells us that on the day after the event, "собрался весь город" (the whole town gathered). Not a single person present wishes to pass judgment on the duel, which has just occurred, mostly because no one seems *to know how to*. On the one hand, Stavrogin is an important member of the town's society, but on the other, he may be insane. Moreover, he has ignored Shatov's grave insult— a slap across the face in front of witnesses. Gaganov himself is also respected in the town. It is not until Yuliya Mikhailovna resorts to an explanation of the situation motivated by class factors that society begins to move. In this time of uncertainty over who is *svoj* in the town, Yuliya makes mention of Shatov's humble beginnings: "Is it really such a surprise that Stavrogin chose to fight Gaganov and ignored the student? He could hardly have challenged his former peasant to a duel!" (272). The narrator's reaction is one of pleased astonishment—not at the originality of Yuliya Mikhailovna's interpretation of events, but at the obviousness of it. Why hadn't anyone else thought of it? "What remarkable words! A clear and simple thought, and yet it had not occurred to anyone up to that point" (272).

With that, a crisis of interpretation for the town's society is averted and Dostoevsky is able to demonstrate the power of the social plane of the *svoj/chuzhoj* opposition. Stavrogin's correct and timely invoking of the opposition, unconscious or not, is able to overcome the gossip that he is insane. The narrator informs us that the affair puts Stavrogin in the town's good graces; he becomes "fashionable" (*on byl v mode*). Yuliya Mikhailovna gains respect in the town for her keen insight, and, most significantly perhaps, Gaganov's act is deemed tactless, but tactless based on the social plane of the *svoj/chuzhoj* opposition:

---

44 Lawrence Kelly, *Diplomacy and Murder in Tehran* (London: I. B. Tauris Publishers, 2002), 52.

"Поступок Артемия Павловича окончательно объявили бестактным: 'своя своих не познаша'"[45] ("Artemii Pavlovich's act was decisively deemed tactless: 'one of us not recognizing his own,'" 272). And perhaps most crucial for Dostoevsky's goals, the student Shatov, previously accepted as *svoj* by the town (he is present for the argument between Praskovya Ivanovna and Varvara Petrovna), is on his way to acquiring the label *chuzhoj*, a status from which he will never recover.

At Our People's

Shatov's expulsion is completed in the chapter entitled "У наших" ("At Our People's Place"). At this nihilist gathering, we first learn of the make-up of the group of five in the provincial town, the men who will go on to murder Shatov in cold blood on the Skvoreshniki estate. Just as importantly, however, we witness an utter breakdown in communication and human interaction, as participants reject out of hand the bonds of familial ties in favor of dubious political ones.

As always, the narrator includes commentary on the quality of the guest list and the presence of several *outsiders* (*postoronnie*), adding that the members of the group of five suspected these outsiders and vice versa. As if this initial tension were not enough, a conflict arises between the political and the familial, a conflict magnified by the fact that this conspiratorial planning session is being held on the same night as a name-day celebration for Virginsky, a member of the group of five. The easy, warm atmosphere one would expect at a name-day celebration is decidedly not present at the Virginsky home. This conflict is exemplified by an exchange between an army major, a close relative of Virginsky's, who encounters his niece, a student and nihilist just returned from St. Petersburg, after ten years of no contact. He is at the event merely to celebrate the name-day; she is there for anything but a celebration. When the major chastises his niece for not sitting like a lady, the young woman refuses to acknowledge their relationship and categorically rejects her uncle's use of the familiar *ty* pronoun:

> "And you shouldn't pop up!" the major blurted out. "You are a young lady, you should behave modestly, and it's as if you sat on a pin."

---

45 The phrase, in Old Church Slavonic, is from the Bible (John 1:11— "He came to his own people, and even they rejected him").

> "Kindly be quiet, and do not dare address me familiarly with your nasty comparisons. It's the first time I have seen you and I do not accept our blood relationship."
> "But I'm your uncle! I used to tote you around in my arms when you were still being breast-fed!"
> "What do I care what you used to tote around? I didn't ask you to tote me around, which means, mister impolite officer, that you got pleasure from it. And allow me to say don't you dare use the familiar address with me, unless it's from civic feeling. I forbid it once and for all." (360)

As the evening continues and several other arguments break out, basic communication begins to collapse. Petty insults are exchanged; more insanity diagnoses are made, and seemingly simple questions are misunderstood. What makes this chaos all the more striking is that it develops against the background of constant reminders from the narrator of all the relatives present. The student/nihilist is Virginsky's wife's sister. Shigalev is her brother. Virginsky's own sister is also present to serve the tea. The major is of course thus related to all of them. The misunderstandings Dostoevsky creates are not accidental, however. The following one allows Madame Virginsky to denigrate family ties even further:

> "Are you really serious?" Madame Virginsky turned to the lame man even somewhat alarmed. "If this man, not knowing what to do about the people, turns nine tenths of them into slavery? I've long suspected him."
> "Your own brother, you mean?" the lame man asked.
> "Family ties? Are you mocking me or not?"

The exchange puts into focus the complete rejection of the interpretation of the *svoj/chuzhoj* opposition on which Grandmother Yankova relied so heavily in the eighteenth and early nineteenth centuries. The nihilists are attempting to effect a change in the opposition at this point, and they are not doing a very good job of it. The criteria for becoming *svoj* are now more socio-political than familial, a shift that may have even warranted a slight change in terminology. Although I have maintained throughout this work that *svoj* and *nash* are almost synonymous when used to evaluate a person, here the latter term most assuredly takes on the political connotations that it carries to this day.[46]

For the nihilists, Aleksandr Herzen's writings stood out as important, and he is mentioned both directly and indirectly at the name-day gathering and in other parts of the novel. In this chapter in particular, we hear mention of Herzen's influential journal *The Bell* (*Kolokol*, 357), a reference to his 1847 novel *Who is to Blame?* (*Kto vinovat?*, 361), and a discussion of the man himself and his political activities (369). In fact, Dostoevsky's dubbing of the conspirators and others in the town as *nashi* was likely inspired by two chapters in Herzen's 1855 work *My Past and Thoughts* (*Byloe i dumy*). Chapter 29 of the work is called "Our People" ("Наши"), while chapter 30, in turn, is called "Not Our People" ("Не наши"). For Herzen, these terms split two groups according to their views on the merits of the West as a model for Russia's future. The pro-West faction, for Herzen, was *nashi*, while the more pro-Russia group (the Slavophiles), was *ne nashi*.

Although the debates between these two groups were often intense, by the time Herzen was writing *My Past and Thoughts*, his mood had mellowed considerably. He praises the Slavophiles almost as often as he criticizes them. In the epigraph to his chapter "Not Our People," Herzen repeats a statement he wrote in an issue of *The Bell* on the occasion of the death of the arch-Slavophile K. S. Aksakov: "Yes, we were their enemies, but we were very strange enemies. We shared one love, but not a lonely one. And, like Janus or the two-headed eagle, as we looked in different directions, the heart that beat within us was the same" (281). Dostoevsky's rather comical depiction of *nashi* seems to poke fun at the categories themselves, and, as we will see in my treatment of Shatov's murder, the author most likely agreed with Herzen's metaphor of the two-headed eagle.

On the subject of Shatov, it is significant that the man in no way participates in the frantic and confused arguing, which escalates as the night continues. His presence is in fact almost forgotten by the narrator, who finally gets around to mentioning him five pages into the chapter: "I have not mentioned Shatov: he was sitting right there at the far corner of the table, his chair moved slightly out of line; he looked down at the ground, was gloomily silent, refused tea and bread, and would not let go of his peaked cap the whole time, as if to show that he had not come for a visit but on business, and could get up and leave whenever he liked" (358).

---

46 There is a present-day political youth group in Russia called *Nashi*. The group, with regional coordinators in St. Petersburg, Voronezh, Tula, Bryansk, and Tambov, is decidedly pro-Kremlin (and financed by the government).

The next mention of Shatov comes at the very end of the chapter when he does finally stand up to take his leave, refusing to answer the question as to whether he would inform the authorities if he knew of a planned political assassination. Interestingly, it is not the narrator who first mentions Shatov's standing up. We learn of it from Virginsky's sister-in-law, who does not even know his name. Shatov is well on his way to becoming fully *chuzhoj*: "'Why is that gentleman getting up?' shouted the female student." Petr Stepanovich calls after Shatov as he leaves the room: "'Shatov, this is not to your advantage!' Vekhovensky shouted after him mysteriously." Shatov deliberately uses the informal *ty* in his reply: "But it is to yours, spy and scoundrel that you are!" Shatov's abrupt departure evokes near hysteria. Note that many of those present have no idea who Shatov is or who invited him. Also note that in the following lines, we do not know whose voices are doing the shouting: "'Who invited him? Who let him in? Who is he? Who is this Shatov? Will he inform on us or not?' the questions poured forth" (374).

Shatov is no longer welcome; even in this almost comically dysfunctional group, he has acquired the label *chuzhoj*. In the next chapter, Stavrogin tells Petr Stepanovich that his group has expertly banished (*otlichno vygnali*) Shatov. In this corrupt society, however, banishment and the status of *chuzhoj* do not lead to a man calling for his carriage. It leads to murder.

The Murder of Shatov

In the chapter preceding the murder, the narrator describes Shatov in the opening pages using some very familiar words: "The disaster with Liza and Marya's death made an overpowering impression on Shatov. I already mentioned that the morning I ran into him he seemed not quite in his right mind (*ne v svoem ume*)" (506) The narrator here uses the very same phrase to characterize Shatov as Sofya uses in *Woe from Wit* to "diagnose" Chatsky as *chuzhoj*/insane and expunge him from Moscow society. With the narrator's comment, Shatov, like Chatsky, has moved further on the— in this case, fatal— path to being forcibly removed from the provincial town's society.

To continue the connections with Griboedov's comedy, the description of the planning of the murder includes phrasings that magnify the dramatic qualities of the crime about to be committed. Later in the chapter the narrator relates how the conspirators "assigned roles" for the upcoming event:

Erkel was the kind of "little fool" whose head lacked only the chief sense; he had no king in his head, but of lesser, subordinate sense he had plenty, even to the point of cunning. Fanatically, childishly devoted to the "common cause" (in actuality, to Petr Stepanovich), he operated according to the instructions given to him by Petr at the meeting at "our people's" house when the roles for the next day were assigned and handed out. Petr Stepanovich assigned him the role of messenger after talking with him for about ten minutes off to the side. The service department was what was required by this shallow, scant-reasoning character, eternally longing to submit to another's will—oh, to be sure, not otherwise than for the sake of a "common" or "great" cause. (514)

In another nod to Griboedov's play, Dostoevsky's narrator begins the chapter in which Shatov is murdered, "Многотрудная ночь" ("A Work-Filled Night") discussing both the breakdown of the family unit and the relaying of gossip, in this instance the very real possibility that Shatov will inform on the group of nihilists. Virginsky, one of the conspirators, spends the day of the murder running around to the houses of all of *nashi* (italics again in the original) trying to convince them that Shatov will most likely not, in fact, inform on them. The reason Virginsky gives for Shatov's change of heart is that his wife has returned and borne him a child. At first reading, it seems that family connections, the original criteria from Grandmother Yankova's time for determining who is *svoj*, have returned to assert their prominence and overrule any concerns Shatov may have about betraying the nihilists. Such an interpretation is undermined, however, when we remember that the child is not Shatov's but Stavrogin's. The family unit is again shown in a weakened state when Virginsky thinks of his wife and how ashamed he is that he is hiding things from her. However, the man is shown as overcome with "a new idea" that occupies his thoughts and actions, and this new idea takes precedence over his relationship with his wife.

The mood shifts significantly as the narrator turns away from society tales of quarrels and accusations to focus the reader's attention on a singular, lonely, and abandoned locale far from the eyes and ears of the townspeople—the Skvoreshniki estate. The passage is exceedingly and startlingly somber, even ominous; while much of the novel up to this point contains satire and sarcasm, the description of the forest and the subsequent murder is devoid of even the smallest attempt at light-heartedness. According to Konstantin Mochulsky in his 1947 *Dostoevsky: His Life and Work* (translated by Michael A. Minihan), the "paysage," as he calls it, appears in Dostoevsky's works when the author is about to relate catastrophic events: "Before the story of the murder, Dostoevsky gives a detailed description of the Skvoreshniki park. The *paysage*, introduced in this scene of great tragic depth, becomes a powerful resonator, heightening the dramatic force of the events. With Dostoevsky, the *paysage* appears only in moments of catastrophe, when delaying the tempo reinforces the tension" (446).

Although Mochulsky's observation does indeed ring true, Dostoevsky was doing something a little different with this particular *paysage*. The description expertly blends space and time as the reader becomes separated from the goings-on in town not only by physical distance; he travels to a time long past and neglected as well.[47]

> Это было очень мрачное место, в конце огромного ставрогинского парка. Я потом нарочно ходил туда посмотреть; как, должно быть, казалось оно угрюмым в тот суровый осенний вечер. Тут начинался старый заказной лес; огромные вековые сосны мрачными и неясными пятнами обозначались во мраке. Мрак был такой, что в двух шагах почти нельзя было рассмотреть друг друга,[48] но Петр Степанович, Липутин, Эркель принесли с собою фонари. Неизвестно для чего и когда, в незапамятное время, устроен был тут из диких нетесаных камней какой-то довольно смешной грот. Стол, скамейки внутри грота давно уже гнили и рассыпались.

---

[47] Gene Moore on the narrator in *Demons*: "Michael Holquist has described *The Possessed* as a 'temporal palimpsest' in the sense that the narrator's chronicle relates events whose sources and motives lie in previous times and distant places. The narrator's story is based on other stories that are not told, but which—to the extent they can be understood at all—must be deciphered and reconstructed from clues that appear as the effects of implied causes" (52).

[48] The narrator's usage of "each other" here is curious in that he claims not to have been at the scene of the crime until the next day, alone presumably. The "each other" gives the impression either that the narrator was there with the conspirators when the crime took place or that they returned the next day with him in tow. It is interesting that as the novel progresses and many characters experience more and more difficulty differentiating between *svoj* and *chuzhoj*, the narrator's role is expanding. He is seen arguing directly with the townspeople and stating his opinion on matters. In effect he is becoming less impartial, more *known* (*svoj*) to the reader. As I mentioned before, according to William Mills Todd III, this type of narrator became popular after the patronage system collapsed in the 1830s. Moreover, critics for years have questioned the narrator's trustworthiness. If he did indeed have something to do with Shatov's murder, Dostoevsky may have been trying to show that this path to *svoj-ness* is just as superficial as blood ties or marriage. At the very least, the phrase adds to the blending of time and space, on which I commented above.

Шагах в двустах вправо оканчивался третий пруд парка. Эти три пруда, начинаясь от самого дома, шли, один за другим, с лишком на версту, до самого конца парка. Трудно было предположить, чтобы какой-нибудь шум, крик или даже выстрел мог дойти до обитателей покинутого ставрогинского дома. Со вчерашним выездом Николая Всеволодовича и с отбытием Алексея Егорыча во всем доме осталось не более пяти или шести человек обитателей, характера, так сказать, инвалидного. Во всяком случае почти с полною вероятностью можно было предположить, что если б и услышаны были кем-нибудь из этих уединившихся обитателей вопли или крики о помощи, то возбудили бы лишь страх, но ни один из них не пошевелился бы на помощь с теплых печей и нагретых лежанок

The place was gloomy in the extreme, situated as it was at the end of the vast Stavrogin park. I later made a special visit to take a look; to see how dismal it must have been on that harsh autumn evening. The old, protected forest began here; the outlines of huge age-old pine trees could be detected as bleak, obscure blurs in the gloom. The gloom was such that it was almost impossible to recognize each other standing just two steps away, but Petr Stepanovich, Liputin, and Erkel had brought along lanterns. In a time long, long, ago someone had built nearby a rather comical grotto out of natural, unhewn stone; when exactly and for what reason, no one knew. The table and benches inside the grotto had long since rotted and crumbled away. About two hundred strides to the right the end of the park's third pond could be made out. These three ponds stretched out one after the other, beginning at the house itself and going up to the very end of the park. It would be hard to imagine any noises or screams, even a gunshot, reaching the inhabitants of the abandoned Stavrogin estate. After the departures of both Nikolai Vsevolodovich and Aleksei Egorich the day before, only five or six occupants—invalids, so to speak—remained in the entire house. In any case, it could be said with full assurance that even if one of these isolated inhabitants did happen to hear a wail or call for help, it would only strike terror in his heart, and not one of them would think to get up from his heated stove-bed to lend a hand. (533)

It is surely not a coincidence that Dostoevsky chose to stage the murder of Shatov where both the urban and the pastoral and the present and the past converge. By exaggerating the references to the society-driven *Woe from Wit*, he reveals the dangers of the purely social interpretation of the *svoj/chuzhoj* opposition and doing so in a description of the most ancient and abandoned forest in the area only serves to drive the point home all the more effectively. By this point in the novel, the paranoia and fear that accompany the painful process of determining who will betray, who will keep the secret, who will fit in, who is *svoj*, have taken hold to such a degree that murder is the only way out. But Dostoevsky is doing more than merely criticizing Russian society's obsession with labeling people *svoj* or *chuzhoj*, he is trying to show the Russian reader the way this opposition once functioned. The murder of Shatov in the shadowy depths of a neglected Russian forest, long forgotten by those who once appreciated it, constitutes a plaintive call for the Russian reader *to remember*.[49]

And thus I ask my reader to remember as well, specifically the ideas expressed in the criticism of the Soviet semioticians, which I mentioned in chapter 1. These articles contain references to just the kind of *svoj/chuzhoj* that Dostoevsky may have meant Shatov to represent.

First of all, Shatov's very name indicates a kind of instability and resistance to stasis. The Russian verb *shatat'* means "to shake, rock, reel, totter," and its reflexive form, *shatat'sya*, describes someone gallivanting, meandering, or wandering, activities in which Shatov certainly has engaged during his transient life. Early on in the novel, the reader receives some telling details concerning Shatov's biography; he was born into poverty, had difficulties fitting in, and refused to remain in one place for long:

> She also did not care for Shatov, who had just the year before become a member of the group. Shatov had been a student earlier and had been expelled from the university after a political indiscretion. He had been a pupil of Stepan Trofimovich's, born a peasant in the servitude of Varvara Petrovna. Shatov's father, now deceased, had been Pavel Fedorov's valet, and Shatov was in Varvara's debt. She did not care for his pride and ingratitude towards her; in no way could she forgive him for not coming to

---

49 Here I agree with Dawn Seckler on the importance of not being too distracted by the political aspects of the novel: "The most political of Dostoevsky's novels and the one most dependent on a particular historical context, *Besy* functions more meaningfully outside of historical time" ("The Absence of Historical Time in Dostoevsky's *Besy*," 58).

her immediately after he was expelled. On the contrary, he did not even reply to her hand-delivered letter, choosing instead to enslave himself to a civilized merchant by teaching the man's children. He traveled abroad with the merchant's family, more as a manservant than a tutor, but he had really wanted to go abroad at the time. There was a governess with the children as well, a lively Russian young lady who was hired by the family right before the trip, chosen more for her low asking price than anything else. About two months later the merchant kicked her out for her "liberal ideas." Shatov shuffled off after her and soon the two had a church wedding in Geneva. They lived together for about three weeks and then parted ways as free souls with no attachments to the other; a lack of funds, of course, also had a hand in it. He then wandered aimlessly around Europe, living as a vagabond on God knows what money. It was said that he was shining shoes on the street corner and working as a porter in some port. (28)

Upon returning to his homeland and the town in which he was born and raised, Shatov continued his poverty-stricken existence, working odd jobs and living alone on the outskirts of town: "He lived alone, at the edge of town..." (30). In another point in the novel, not only is he described as having two aspects to his personality, he is also compared to a bear:[50]

> The clumsy, bashful Shatov was not one for tender attentions. A coarse man on the outside, on the inside he seemed quite delicate. Although he would often go overboard, it was he himself who would suffer the most afterwards. After growling something under his breath at Stepan Trofimovich's plea for reconciliation and stamping his feet in place like a bear, he would suddenly smirk, put aside his coat, and sit back down, staring obstinately at the ground. (37)

In their article on the opposition, Ivanov and Toporov mark the bear as a link between the *svoj* and *chuzhoj* elements; it acts as a kind of human/animal hybrid: "The bear may act as a positive entity whose nature is humanoid and

---

50 In Russian, a bear that does not hibernate is called a *medved'-shatun*, a "wanderer bear," because it wanders during the winter and does not settle in one spot.

who possesses a soul, thanks to its former existence as a human ['one of us']" (160). Perhaps just as important as the connection between Shatov and a bear is Dostoevsky's description of him as a person exhibiting a complex duality, someone who conceivably could be both *svoj and chuzhoj* at the same time. In Dostoevsky's mind, these types are often shunned.

As I stated in chapter 1, the semioticians have asserted that at one time in the pre-Petrine period there existed a less strict boundary between the two poles of the opposition, with Lotman and Uspensky in particular pointing to sorcerers, shamans, and possessors of special knowledge as individuals who may be perceived as both *svoj* and *chuzhoj*:

> Heuristically, one could consider the situation of an ancestral society that places a certain ambiguity into the concept of "alien, stranger, outsider" as a point of departure. On the one hand, an "alien, outsider, stranger" is someone who has arrived from without, an enemy, or a metek, one who has been deprived of the full range of societal rights and resides on "our" territory but belongs to some other world from which he has arrived. On the other hand, shamans, sorcerers, and prophets are "one of us—alien, outsider, stranger" who simultaneously belong to both "our" (terrestrial) world and the "alien, foreign" afterworld. In the first instance, the "alien, outsider, stranger" is an object of enmity or protection and in the second one of fear and respect. This creates the possibility for a psychological swap in the collective's treatment of the two given, heterogeneous groups: one could perceive in every alien/outsider/stranger a sorcerer and treat him with wary respect. One could also regard even a gentile shaman or sorcerer with as much suspicion as one would regard an agent of hostile neighbors. (110)

Shatov also shares other characteristics with the *izgoj* described earlier: he lives on the outskirts of town and has led a vagabond life. I will cite again a quotation I first presented in chapter 1, this time specifically with Shatov in mind (note the use of the verb *shatat'sya*): "Человек, находящийся 'вне', выключен из социальных структур, пространственно он проживает *вне*—вне дома, шатаясь по улицам и ночуя под заборами (или в кабаках, в новое время на вокзалах, которые *не жилье*), странствуя по дорогам, живя в лесу или на кладбище или селясь за городской чертой" ("A person who is on 'the outside,' is excluded from social structures; spatially he lives *outside*—outside of home, roaming the streets and sleeping under fences (or in taverns, in modern times in railway stations, which are *not* lodging), wandering the roads, residing in the forest or in graveyards or settling outside the city limits," 116).

The word *izgoj* technically refers to a person who has changed his social status, especially in Kievan Rus'. The *Oxford Russian-English Dictionary* defines an *izgoj* as a "person in Kievan Russian Society with changed status; e.g. illiterate son of a priest, ruined merchant, freed slave (167)." This definition is followed by the figurative meaning "social odd man out." Dostoevsky certainly appreciated the type in his novels, and in *Demons* he actually provides a rather long description of what seems to be a group of *izgois* in the first pages of the chapter "Праздник. Отдел первый" ("The Party, Part 1"). The narrator is explaining just what kind of "people" (he uses the pejorative diminutive *lyudishki*) had begun to gain influence in the provincial town as the literary quadrille approached:

> And yet the trashiest of filth suddenly gained influence among us and began loudly criticizing all that is holy, when before they wouldn't have dared open their mouths. And the prominent people in town, to this point so successfully reigning supreme, suddenly began to listen to them and not speak their minds. Others began even to snicker in the most shameful of fashions. The upper hand was now being seized by all sorts of trash—people with names like Lyamshin and Telyatnikov, but also the Tentetnikovs who owned land, and those homegrown milksops, the Radishchevs. Then there were the little heebs with their mournful but haughty smiles, the fun-loving travelers stopping in, the poets with a radical tendency from the capital, and the poets, who, in place of a tendency or talent, had peasant coats and tarred boots. There were also majors and colonels who sneered at their own positions and were prepared to give up their swords and sneak off in the night to become railroad clerks for an extra ruble, generals defecting to become the lawyers, politically correct dealers, developing little merchants, countless seminarians, and women who personified the woman question. These people had the upper hand, but over whom? (417)

For Lotman and Uspensky, the *izgoj* also sometimes possesses secret knowledge. The authors describe a special type of *izgoi*, the *razboiniki*, or bandits, and claim that they were thought to possess special knowledge about the location of buried treasure.⁵¹ Again, I repeat the quote from chapter 1: "Among the wide range of activities in which bandits typically involved themselves were such acts of mysticism and wizardry as the burying and search for treasure. Innumerable are the legends that connect the ataman bandits and Cossacks with the secrets of booty, stories of buried or found treasure and the secret methods of recovering it from beneath the ground" (117).

To return to the chapter of *Demons* under discussion, if we remove all the political trappings of the story concerning terrorism and the overthrow of the government, what we are left with, at least toward the end of the novel, is the tale of a man invited into the woods to unearth some buried treasure, a printing press. No one but Shatov possesses the knowledge of its location. Moreover, the nihilists employ the same method to signal one another as the bandits. According to Lotman and Uspensky, the bandits' preferred method of signaling one another is the whistle: "The whistle is the characteristic warning signal used by bandits [the whistle was traditionally considered to draw the attention of dark forces]. The whistle is a sort of bandit 'uniform,' the distinguishing sign by which other people recognize him" (118).

The nihilists learn of Shatov's approach into the grotto also by means of the whistle: "Right at that moment, at a distance of about two hundred strides, they heard a whistle coming from the pond side of the park. Liputin immediately answered the whistle with one of his own (that morning, not confident of the abilities of his toothless mouth, he had bought a child's whistle made of clay for a kopeck). Erkel had managed to warn Shatov as they walked that there would be whistling so that he did not suspect anything" (538).

Although Dostoevsky had obviously not read the semioticians of the twentieth century, he was most definitely in tune with the topics on which they wrote. If the "folk" interpretation of Shatov's murder seems far-fetched to some, it might help to point out that Dostoevksy was indeed interested in and knowledgeable about the realms of fairy-tale and folk-lore. In *Demons*, perhaps the most obvious nod to this world is the character of Marya Lebyadkina, the lame, half-wit sister of Captain Lebyadkin. Konstantin Mochulsky comments on her:

---

51 As a little boy, Dostoevsky fell in love with Friedrich Schiller's play *Die Räuber* ("Разбойники," *The Bandits*). Nina Koroleva writes: "As a ten-year-old boy, F. M. Dostoevsky was brought to Moscow's Maly Theatre. The first impressions left by Molchalov's performance in Schiller's *The Bandits* were so strong that he could not forget them literally for the rest of his life. Schiller's drama *The Bandits* was one of the first works with which Fyodor Mikhailovich began to read to his children" (125).

> She is depicted most realistically: the feeble-minded, mistreated sister of Captain Lebyadkin, a girl of about thirty, with an emaciated face and quiet, kindly gray eyes; a cripple and a holy fool; but at the same time all these qualifications: outward appearance, costume, circumstances, social position—appear fantastic. Under them glimmers another reality, a different mystical plane of being. Marya Timofeyevna is the beautiful maiden, the bride of folk tales. On the table before her is an old pack of cards, a rustic mirror and a worn-out copy of a song book. She also speaks in "fairy tales." (465)

Furthermore, in a conversation between Marya and Shatov, the woman admits to being able to tell the future by means of the aforementioned pack of cards and that at least one "respectable" member of the town has come by to have her fortune read.

And then there is the character of Tolkachenko, one of Shatov's murderers, who has made a living observing and studying bandits and scoundrels and their way of life:

> Now that it is no longer a secret, these men were, first off, Liputin, then Verkhovensky himself, long-eared Shpigalev—the brother of Mrs. Virginsky, Lyamshin, and, finally, a certain Tolkachenko. This Tolkachenko, a strange character of about forty, was known for his immense knowledge of the common people, especially the ways of swindlers and bandits. He spent his time going from tavern to tavern (not only to study the common man, by the way) standing out among us with his cheap clothes, tarred boots, studiedly sly approach, and the folk phrases he sprinkled enthusiastically into every conversation. (356)

After Shatov finally informs the others as to the location of the printing press, it is Tolkachenko who makes the first lunge at him (as if his extra knowledge of rogues and bandits has come in handy). In a sense, then, the nihilists are merely posing as bandits (remember, roles have been assigned for this mission). They are [ab]using their knowledge of folklore to catch and kill the real bandit, the real shaman, the one who knows things—Ivan Shatov. The following is the powerful account of Shatov's murder, (note again the use of the word for scene/stage in describing the events):[52]

> Теперь совершенно известно до малейших подробностей, как произошло это ужасное происшествие. Сначала Липутин встретил Эркеля и Шатова у самого грота; Шатов с ним не раскланялся и не подал руки, но тотчас же торопливо и громко произнес:
>
> —Ну, где же у вас заступ и нет ли еще другого фонаря? Да не бойтесь, тут ровно нет никого, и в Скворешниках теперь, хотя из пушек отсюдова пали, не услышат. Это вот здесь, вот тут, на самом этом месте . . .
>
> И он стукнул ногой действительно в десяти шагах от заднего угла грота, в стороне леса. В эту самую минуту бросился сзади на него из-за дерева Толкаченко, а Эркель схватил его сзади же за локти. Липутин накинулся спереди. Все трое тотчас же сбили его с ног и придавили к земле. Тут подскочил Петр Степанович с своим револьвером. Рассказывают, что Шатов успел повернуть к нему голову и еще мог разглядеть и узнать его. Три фонаря освещали сцену. Шатов вдруг прокричал кратким и отчаянным криком; но ему кричать не дали: Петр Степанович аккуратно и твердо наставил ему револьвер прямо в лоб, крепко в упор и—спустил курок

The events of that horrible evening are now well-known, even down to the most trivial detail. First off, Liputin met Erkel and Shatov at the edge of the grotto. Shatov did not bow or offer to shake hands. He rushed in and in a hasty and loud voice asked:

"So, where's the shovel and do you have another lantern? Come on, don't get scared on me. There's no one here. These days you could shoot a cannonball in Skvoreshniki and no one would hear it. It's right here, right on this spot . . ."

He tapped his foot actually ten steps from the back corner of the grotto, in the direction of the forest. At that very moment Tolkachenko leapt out at him from behind a tree and Erkel

---

52 Again, keep in mind that Griboedov was also murdered by a group of people. An angry mob stormed the Russian embassy in Tehran where the author-turned-diplomat was serving.

grabbed him by the elbows from the rear. Liputin attacked from the front. The three of them knocked Shatov off his feet and pressed him into the ground. Petr Stepanovich then jumped out with his revolver. The story goes that Shatov had enough time to turn his head and recognize him. Three lanterns illuminated the scene [stage]. Shatov suddenly let out a brief scream of despair. But the scream was cut short: Petr Stepanovich carefully and firmly pointed the revolver directly at Shatov's forehead. At point blank range, he pulled the trigger. (539)

Ivanov and Toporov claim (158–161) that occasionally in East Slavic fairy tales and folk songs the bear acts in opposition not only to humans but to fire as well, and the authors point the reader to the many instances of interaction between the Medved' and water. They quote a fortune-telling song (*podblyudnaya pesnya*), in which a bear is swimming along a river, and a fairy tale in one of Afanas'ev's works in which a bear drowns in one. After Petr Stepanovich kills Shatov, the group of men ties rocks to his corpse and throws it into the third pond on the Skvoreshniki grounds.[53]

With this single gunshot, Petr Stepanovich has managed to eliminate the bandit, the outcast, the sorcerer, and the bear from Russian soil. But that is not the worst of it. Dostoevsky has also shown the reader that with this one murder, an entire method of interpreting the *svoj/chuzhoj* opposition has also been eradicated. If a reliance on a purely social interpretation of the *svoj/chuzhoj* opposition led to the banishment and "insanity" of Aleksandr Chatsky in *Woe*

---

53 Dostoevsky may have had intended an even more "folk" interpretation of Shatov's demise. Orlando Figes points out that the Russian peasantry often strongly believed in a heaven on earth, specifically on Russian soil. Considering that Shatov, an ultra-nationalist and former peasant, believes in Russia but not in God, Dostoevsky may have dispatched him to find faith in this heavenly place, which, significantly, was often thought to be located under a lake: "The peasantry believed in a Kingdom of God on this earth. Many of them conceived of heaven as an actual place in some remote corner of the world, where the rivers flowed with milk and the grass was always green. This conviction inspired dozens of popular legends about a real Kingdom of God hidden in the Russian land. There were legends of the Distant Lands, of the Golden Islands, of the Kingdom of Opona, and the Land of Chud', a sacred kingdom underneath the ground where the 'White Tsar' ruled according to 'ancient and truly just ideals' of the peasantry. The oldest of these folk myths was the legend of Kitezh—a sacred city that was hidden underneath the lake of Svetloyar (in Nizhegorodskaya Province) and was only visible to the true believers of the Russian faith" (308). Yuri Stepanov pointed out in his section on the *svoj/chuzhoj* opposition that Chud' is one possible etymology for the word *chuzhoj* and that the Chud' peoples were consistently regarded by Russians as sorcerers and magicians, all of whom represent both types of *izgoi* and less negative representatives of *chuzhie lyudi*.

from Wit, here it has led to murder. The *izgois* of Russia, the bandits and the rogues, the sorcerers and the shamans, perfectly illustrated both a less rigid divide between the two poles of the opposition and a less worldly, society-based evaluation of its components. Without them and what they represent, Dostoevsky is saying, Russia will only suffer.

In Place of a Conclusion

I would like to use this space to highlight what is taking place today, in 2021, when it comes to the *svoj-chuzhoj* opposition. There can be no doubt that Russian speakers continue to make strong distinctions between these two poles. The words and the concepts they represent still travel hand-in-hand and are encountered at all levels of discourse. If only one of the two poles is mentioned, the other's absence is felt. Fyodor Dostoevsky's appeal in the novel *Demons* for a more nuanced and situational interpretation of the dynamic has seemingly gone unheeded. If we recall, the sociologist Anna Shor-Chudnovskaya described Russians as being on a *life-long quest* to find a group of people to call their own. But this quest naturally contains another component: the need to avoid being perceived as *chuzhoj*. A survey conducted by Shor-Chudnovskaya, which the researcher shared with me by email, provides insight into why. Two hundred university students in St. Petersburg were asked to respond to precise inquiries concerning the terms *svoj* and *chuzhoj*. When asked how they interpreted the negative pole of the opposition, the students replied:

- "*Chuzhoj* is a person who has nothing in common with us or me."
- "People don't know someone who is *chuzhoj*, and do not help him as much as they would someone who is *svoj*."
- "*Chuzhoj* may pose a danger to us. We do not know what to expect from him and we don't know what kind of a person he is."

The key term in these responses is the verb *to know*. Russians seek to know a person, to know how he will react in all situations, to be able to *predict*. Unpredictability equals danger and very likely betrayal. This foundation for forming close relationships is not a flawed one—after all, who would want to be betrayed? The problem lies in the concomitant worldview, one that interprets *all* people outside of one's close circle as potential betrayers. This tendency compels groups of *svoi lyudi* to close ranks and implicitly conveys to its members that *remaining* a member of this group is more important than anything else. Cherishing the group, even fetishizing it, is the entire point of its existence and what keeps it going. Such activities as involvement in civil society, even employment, are secondary. This single-mindedness in approaching interpersonal relations is fraught and can have a negative impact on more neutral, transactional interactions such as mitigating the effects of widespread disasters, where dependence on neighbors and even strangers is essential.

Additionally, in the corporate world, Russian executives and employees at all levels are inclined to view their coworkers and subordinates as family members; this practice has the potential to stunt the growth and effectiveness of the enterprise. In an article entitled "Svoi i Chuzhie: Kak semeistvennost' raz"edaet rossiiskie kompanii" ("One's Own and Not One's Own: How Nepotism Eats Away at Russian Companies"), Valentina Uralova describes this management style as a purely Russian one:

> Когда мы, сервис-дизайнеры, приходим в российские компании, то часто слышим: "мы одна семья", "своих не сдаем". За этим фразами скрывается культурный феномен семейственности—стойкий социальный паттерн, мешающий развиваться среднему и крупному бизнесу. Феномен чисто российский, связанный с властью и нарушением личных границ.
>
> As soon as we service designers arrive at a Russian company's headquarters, we're told, "we're one big family here," or "we do not leave *svoi* behind." These sentiments are in line with the cultural phenomenon of nepotism—a pervasive social pattern that hinders large and average-sized businesses from growing. The phenomenon, strictly a Russian one, is all about control and the violation of personal boundaries.[54]

Perhaps one of the most impersonal relationships in a society is the one between a government and its people. Russians view its leadership class not as neutral, however, but as *chuzhoj*. They have little desire to interact with the country's elites; they do not know them and will never know them. They are thus essentially writing off an entire portion of society, a decision that then allows their leaders to act with little participation from the people. In fact, the Russian government, left to its own devices, has seized on the *svoj/chuzhoj* opposition and is exploiting it to the utmost. Once the people of a nation decide that its

---

54 Valentina Uralova, "Svoi i Chuzhie: Kak semeistvennost' raz"edaet rossiiskie kompanii," RBK Pro, https://pro.rbc.ru/news/5d8e04af9a79477895a13c88.

government is made up of people with whom no one would want to associate, it cedes a great deal of power and decision-making to this *chuzhoj* entity. The result, then, is that the Putin regime is free to use these very same terms as a cudgel to advance its aims.

The government, especially since the terrorist attacks in Moscow (2002) and Beslan (2004), the color revolutions of the mid-2000s, and the "August conflict" with Georgia in 2008, has exhibited an almost laser-like focus on the dichotomy, safe in the knowledge that they are in command of its interpretation. The regime has at its disposal a powerful rhetorical tool, one firmly entrenched in the culture and language themselves, for dividing and separating people, groups, even entire cultures, into categories.

The Putin regime employs slickly produced documentaries made by the likes of Arkady Mamontov and Aleksandr Rogatkin, directors whose films lack subtlety in driving home their point: our enemies are *chuzhoj*. The titles of a series of made-for-television documentaries made by Mamontov and Rogatkin speak for themselves: *Chuzhie, Svoj-chuzhoj, Svoi lyudi, Chuzhie?*

The first of these films chronologically is from a larger project of Mamontov's entitled *Obratnaya storona* (*The Flip Side*). The online description of the forty-five-minute film reads:

> Терроризм в переводе с латинского языка значит "ужас". К сожалению, в нашей стране ужас стал повседневным явлением. В 1999 году в стране было зарегистрировано 20 террористических актов, в 2000 году 135, в 2001 году 300. Тысячи людей погибли и были ранены. В нашу страну вторглись чужие, это люди, которые ненавидят нас, они хотят только одного—уничтожить всех, кто думает иначе, чем они.[55]

> Terrorism translated from the Latin means "terror." Unfortunately, terror has become an everyday occurrence in our country. In 1999, 20 terrorist attacks were committed in the country, 135 in 2000, and 300 in 2001. Thousands of people have died or been wounded. Our country is being overrun by outsiders. These are people who hate us. They want only one thing—to destroy anyone who thinks differently than they do.

---

[55] "Chuzhie. Naemniki na Kavkaze (Rossiya) 2006 god," October 7, 2015, shtab.su/video/rf/vtoraya-chechenskaya-vojna/chuzghie_naemniki_na_kavkaze_smotret_onlayn.html.

This alarmist description of the state of world affairs was something encountered in many countries and cultures after September 11. In fact, if you called it a standard "us vs. them" call to arms, you wouldn't be incorrect. The difference in the Russian context, however, lies in the use and the power of the word *chuzhie*. My translation of the word as "outsiders" is weak. The Russian word produces an unsettling effect in a native speaker, which most any translation into English fails to convey. The word suggests something hidden, something at times unrecognizable, something that has infiltrated the space where one should feel safe. At the same time, however, it implies something possibly once familiar, which has gone on to betray us. It is no coincidence that the word is used so frequently in both the titles and in the overall narration of the Mamontov and Rogatkin propaganda films. Again, the directors' use of the word both registers and plays up the fear in Russian society of being perceived as *chuzhoj*.

As I have mentioned, the implementation of the "us vs. them" conceit hardly constitutes something novel in speaking about most anything, and especially when the subject is international terrorism. But Mamontov in particular weaponizes the opposition in a manner that would be difficult to imagine in other cultures. He blames not Islam as a whole for the terrorist attacks in Russia, but what he refers to as "foreign Islam" (*zarubezhnyi islam*). This "foreign Islam" is juxtaposed to what the filmmaker and others refer to as "domestic/homegrown [Russian] Islam" (*otechestvennyi islam*). The outsiders, according to Mamontov, appeared in Russia in 1995. They settled in Chechnya and Dagestan in particular, infiltrating the local culture and espousing radical ideas. But they were never accepted fully. Of the main protagonist of the film, Mamontov says "Он женился на местной девушке, но все равно остался чужим" (He married a local girl, but nevertheless remained an outsider).

It is interesting to note that in the particular scenario put forth by Mamontov, the group of "one's own" (*svoi*) that is being infiltrated includes naïve, non-(ethnically) Russian residents. Mamontov's purpose seems to be to elicit the maximum level of fear in the viewer, an effect accomplished through the constant use of the word *chuzhie*. The "flip side" of the use of the opposition is to arouse sympathy and a feeling of solidarity with the supposedly innocent citizens of Chechnya and Dagestan. It presumably evokes nostalgia in the Russian viewer for a time when the USSR looked after the citizens of its less fortunate and less powerful republics.

The documentary outlines how these outside forces opened educational institutions and community centers in the former republics under the guise of providing aid to the country through philanthropic work. Mamontov claims that one institution in particular, the "Society for Social Reform" (Общество социальных реформ), is ubiquitous in the former republics of Central Asia and the Caucasus: "В каждом регионе существует свой центр. Например, город Бишкек. Киргизия. Здесь обществом построен университет. Перечисляются огромные деньги для помощи нищим собратьям" ("Each region has its own center. For example, the city of Bishkek, Kyrgyzstan. The people have opened a university here. Large sums of money are sent to aid their poverty-stricken brethren," "Chuzhie. Naemniki na Kavkaze"). The university in Bishkek is called "Kyrgyz-Kuwait University," and a department head states in an interview that the institution employs teachers from across the Muslim world. The Kyrgyz students, these "poverty-stricken brethren," are indeed Muslim, but they practice the above-mentioned *otechestvennyi, mirolyubivyi islam* (domestic, peace-loving Islam), which the outsiders are trying to supplant.

As the documentary progresses, the word *chuzhie* is heard more and more often, while the word *terroristy* (terrorists) is used only occasionally. If a documentary such as this were to be made in English (or perhaps any other language), the word "terrorist" would suffice as a descriptor. The word "terrorist" would elicit the requisite level of revulsion and fear in the viewer. But in Russian-speaking cultures, the word *chuzhoj* is clearly more forceful than the word "terrorist." Mamontov knows this, and by the end of his film, we no longer hear anything at all about "terrorists." We hear about "банды чужих" (gangs of outsiders) and "базы чужих" (outsider bases). When a young Chechen man admits to shooting three Russian women at point-blank range with a pistol at the behest of his terrorist mentors, the narrator does not call him a murderer or a terrorist. He calls him *chuzhoj*: "Этот парень уже чужой. Настоящий чужой. Без тени сомнения в глазах. С руками по локоть в крови" (This guy is already an outsider. A true outsider. Not the slightest bit of doubt in his eyes, up to the elbows in blood).

As the documentary reaches its conclusion, the narrator starts to repeat the word *chuzhoj* over and over, a powerful aural assault on the viewer.

Another crucial characteristic of these outsiders is that they are, and always have been, according to the documentary, homeless, or rather homeland-less ("без родины"). And because they have no home of their own, they are trying to infiltrate someone else's and impose foreign values on it. It is this threat that is so dramatically portrayed in the documentary. Yes, they are terrorists, and the film begins with a definition of the word from the Latin. But in the minds of the filmmakers, terrorism on Russian soil is perhaps not as frightening as an invasion of different/foreign/alien thoughts and ideals. They do not blame religion, for it is not Islam that is a threat, it is "foreign/alien Islam." They do not blame race, either, for it is not those with Turkic or Arabic blood that are a threat, it is those

Arabs who are from somewhere else, who are without a homeland, and who have possibly spent some time in the West.

Again, this rhetorical and linguistic tool is unique to Russian speakers; its equivalent is distinctly missing in other languages and cultures. The word *chuzhoj*, taught to generations of students learning Russian in the English-speaking world to mean simply "someone else's, a stranger's," evokes a powerful uneasiness in those born and raised in the culture. The antonym *svoj*, on the other hand, still operates in the Russian-speaking world as one of the highest of compliments that can be bestowed on someone. These distinctions are difficult to grasp to those with only a cursory familiarity with Russia and Russians.

The Russian government is able to apply this linguistic and cultural weapon to most any group or individual if it fits its narrative. The title of another Mamontov television documentary, this one from 2009, contains both elements of the opposition: *Svoj-chuzhoj*. The subject matter this time is the so-called "August conflict" of 2008 between Russia and Georgia, a well-known topic for anyone from the former Soviet Union. The lens for Mamontov's task is the familiar opposition of the title, but in this case, at least initially, it is also the name of a radar-locating system from Soviet times used to distinguish enemy assets from friendly ones. In English this system is most often referred to as the System for Identifying Friend or Foe. The words in Russian, however, carry a much heavier semantic load, and the ambiguity is exploited to maximum effect in the film. Mamontov expands on the concrete purposes of the Friend or Foe system and states provocatively: "У военных есть такое понятие: *свой-чужой*, когда в ракеты и в самолеты закладываются специальные системы и коды опознавания—когда стрелять или не стрелять, кто свой или чужой. В августе 2008 года, все коды были сбиты, и свои стали чужими" (In the military there is a concept known as *friend or foe*, when missiles and aircraft are equipped with a special system and identification codes—when to shoot and when not to, who is a friend and who is a foe. In August 2008, these codes were destroyed, and friends [*svoi*] became foes [*chuzhie*]).

This last line refers to Ukraine and the director's goal is to show how the country was involved in the 2008 conflict; Kyiv (and, to a lesser extent, the United States, Turkey, and Israel) allegedly provided assistance to the Georgians. The people interviewed in the film claim that it was indeed the Ukrainians who supplied the Georgians with the training, equipment, and weaponry necessary to wage war against the Russians. At least once in the documentary, a Russian military officer refers to Ukrainians as "наши братья" (our brothers): the implication being that supplying the enemy with training and weaponry is a treasonous act, a betrayal of their previous *svoj* status. What is left out of this equation is that Georgia, also a former Soviet republic, could also lay claim to this *svoj* status. In Mamontov's use of the opposition in this particular film, however, Georgians are left out of that part of Soviet history.

More recently, as the Covid-19 pandemic began to upend the world, the Putin regime took to employing the positive pole of the opposition in its propaganda campaigns. It turns out that the term *svoj* can be just as persuasive as the ominous *chuzhoj*. In early 2020, the Russian government created a widely disseminated slogan—"своих не бросаем"[56] (we do not abandon our own)—to demonstrate its resolve to help citizens stranded abroad due to travel restrictions. The saying took off, morphed into a popular hashtag, and is now closely associated with Putin, who is alleged to have once uttered the phrase in public. Several websites are now selling T-shirts with the slogan printed below a photograph of the Russian president. The *svoi* here are Russian citizens, any Russian citizens, and the *meaning* of the slogan is translated easily into any language. It has been rendered in English as "No man left behind," a translation perfectly adequate for most situations. It does not, however, convey the sense of patriotism, of duty, and, most importantly, of pride of membership in a group that the Russian original demonstrates through one simple but effective word: *svoi*.

There is a battle looming in Russian society, which will involve to no small degree a conflict over the interpretation of the *svoj/chuzhoj* opposition. If the Russian people continue to view the government as utterly *chuzhoj*, the elites in the country are free to use these terms, especially on the ethnic level, in any way they see fit. They are able to define patriotism, citizenship, and betrayal. At the present time, the Russian people believe they are the ultimate arbiters of the issue and they hold the methods of inquiry used to identify *svoi* in the highest regard. On the journey to find a group of one's own, to *know* someone, knowledge becomes performative and situational— knowledge as talking and interacting rather than knowledge as doing or instructing. The clan knows *people*, not facts; reactions, not secrets; faults, not locations. Human predictability is welcomed. Yes, they know the government is lying to its people, but it can be argued that Russians are already primed and willing, to a certain extent, to ignore what the government is saying, true or untrue. The truth for a Russian speaker is to be found in human interaction with a select few and as long as this group of one's own exists, the outside world is free to do as it pleases. Russian speakers would do well to expand their expectations of truth.

---

56 The phrase is from the Russian film *Brat 2* (*Brother 2*), where it appears in a slightly different form. The main character, Danila Bagrov, played by Sergei Bodrov Jr, tells the prostitute Dasha, "Русские на войне своих не бросают" (Russians do not abandon their own during a war). *Brat 2*, dir. Aleksei Balabanov, https://vimeo.com/459777920 (at the 1:35:47 mark).

Bibliography

Primary Sources

Dostoevsky, Fyodor [F. M. Dostoevskii]. *Zapisnye tetradi*. Moscow and Leningrad: Akademiia, 1935.

———. *The Notebooks for "The Possessed."* Translated by Victor Terras. Edited by Edward Wasiolek. Chicago: The University of Chicago Press, 1968.

———. *The Gambler with Polina Suslova's Diary*. Translated by Victor Terras. Edited by Edward Wasiolek. Chicago: The University of Chicago Press, 1972.

——— [F. M. Dostoevskii]. *Besy*. Moscow: Eksmo-Press, 2002.

———. *Demons*. Translated by Richard Pevear and Larisa Volokhonsky. New York: Alfred A. Knopf, Inc., 1994.

Griboedov, Alexander. *Woe from Wit*. Translated and commentary by Mary Hobson. Lewiston, New York: The Edwin Mellen Press, 2005.

——— [A. S. Griboedov]. *Polnoe sobranie sochinenii*. Vol. 3. Edited by N. K. Piksanov. Petrograd: Razriad iziashchnoi slovesnosti Akademii Nauk, 1917.

———. *Gore ot uma*. Introduction and notes by D. P. Costello. Letchworth, Herts, Great Britain: Prideaux Press, 1983.

——— [A. S. Griboedov]. *Dramaticheskie sochineniia, stikhotvoreniia, stat'i, putevye zametki*. St. Petersburg: Notabene, 1999.

——— [A. S. Griboedov]. *Gore ot uma*. Edited by N. K. Piksanov. Moscow: Nauka, 1969.

Herzen, A. I. *Byloe i dumy*. Vol. 2. Petrograd: Slovo, 1921.

Lermontov, M. Iu. "Smert' poeta." In his *Sochineniia v dvukh tomakh*, vol. 1, 157–159. Moscow: Pravda, 1988.

Leskov, N. S. "Chertogon." In his *Sobranie sochinenii*, vol. 6, 302–210. Moscow: Gosudarstvennoe izdatel' stvo khudozhestvennoi literatury, 1957.

Pushkin, Aleksandr [A. S. Pushkin]. *Polnoe sobranie sochinenii v desiati tomakh*. Vol. 7: *Kritika i publitsistika*. Leningrad: Nauka, 1978.

——— [A. S. Pushkin]. *Evgenii Onegin. Proza*. Moscow: Eksmo, 2002.

―――. *The Complete Works of Alexander Pushkin—Critical and Autobiographical Prose.* Edited by Ian Sproat. Vol. 13. Norfolk, Great Britain: Milner and Company Limited, 2003.

Radishchev, A. N. *Puteshestvie iz Peterburga v Moskvu.* Moscow: Goslitizdat, 1949.

Rasskazy babushki iz vospominanii piati pokolenii, zapisannye i sobrannye ee vnukom D. Blagovo. Edited by T. I. Ornatskaia. Leningrad: Nauka, 1989.

Suslova, Apollinaria. *Gody blizosti s Dostoevskim.* New York: Serebrianyi vek, 1982.

Tolstoy, L. N. *Anna Karenina.* Moscow: Eksmo-Press, 2001.

Secondary Sources

Allain, Louis. "Fyodor Dostoevsky as Bearer of a Nationalistic Outlook." In *The Search for Self-Definition in Russian Literature*, edited by Ewa Thompson, 138–149. Houston, Texas: Rice University Press, 1991.

Aronson, M., and S. Reizer. *Literaturnye kruzhki i salony.* Leningrad: Priboi, 1929.

Ashukin, N. S., and M. G. Ashukina. *Krylatye slova.* Moscow: Khudozhestvennoe izdatel'stvo, 1955.

Bem, A. L. "Dostoevskii—genial'nyi chitatel'." In *O Dostoevskom: Sbornik statei*, edited by A. L. Bem, 5–22. Paris: Amga Editions, 1986.

Berreby, David. *Us and Them: Understanding your Tribal Mind.* New York: Little, Brown and Company, 2005.

Blok, A. A. "O drame." http://blok.lit-info.ru/blok/kritika/o-drame.htm.

Dal', Vladimir. *Poslovitsy russkogo naroda.* Moscow: Gosudarstvennoe izdatel'stvo khudozhestvennoi literatury, 1957.

Driver, Sam. *Pushkin: Literature and Social Ideas.* New York: Columbia University Press, 1989.

Fasmer, M. *Etimologicheskii slovar' russkogo iazyka.* Moscow: Astrel', 2003.

Figes, Orlando. *Natasha's Dance.* New York: Metropolitan Books, 2002.

Fomichev, S. A. "'Gore ot uma' v perspektive 'zolotogo veka' russkoi literatury." In *Vek nyneshnii i vek minuvshii...*, 404–414. St. Petersburg: Azbuka-Klassika, 2002.

Gershenzon, M. *Griboedovskaia Moskva.* Moscow: M. i S. Sabashnikovy, 1914.

Gibian, George. "How Russian Proverbs Present the Russian Character." In *Russianness—In Honor of Rufus Mathewson, 1918–1978*, 38–43. Ann Arbor: Ardis Publishers, 1990.

Golburt, Luba. *The First Epoch*. Madison, Wisconsin: The University of Wisconsin Press, 2014.

Granovetter, Mark S. "The Strength of Weak Ties." *American Journal of Sociology* 76, no. 6 (1973): 1360–1380.

Handbook of Russian Literature. Edited by Victor Terras. New Haven, Connecticut: Yale University Press, 1985.

Ivanov, V, and V. N. Toporov. *Slavianskie iazykovye modeliruiushchie semioticheskie sistemy (drevnii period)*. Moscow: Nauka, 1965.

Janecek, Gerald. "A Defense of Sof'ja in Woe from Wit." *Slavic and East European Journal* 21, no. 3 (Autumn 1977): 318–331.

Karlinsky, Simon. *Russian Drama from its Beginnings to the Age of Pushkin*. Berkeley, California: University of California Press, 1985.

Kelly, Lawrence. *Diplomacy and Murder in Tehran*. London: I. B. Tauris Publishers, 2002.

Koroleva, N. "Dostoevskii i 'Gore ot uma.'" In *Dostoevskii i teatr*, 118–153. Leningrad: Iskusstvo, 1983.

Lebedev, A. *Griboedov: fakty i gipotezy*. Moscow: Iskusstvo, 1980.

Lotman, Iu. M., and B.A. Uspenskii. "Izgoi i izgoinichestvo kak sotsial'no-psikhologicheskaia pozitsiia v russkoi literature preimushchestvenno dopetrovskogo perioda." In *Istoriia i tipologiia russkoi kul'tury*, 222–232. St. Petersburg: Iskusstvo-SPb, 2002.

Lubensky, Sophia. *Russian-English Dictionary of Idioms*. New York: Random House, 1995.

Martinsen, Deborah A. *Surprised by Shame*. Columbus, Ohio: The Ohio State University Press, 2003.

Meerson, Olga. *Dostoevsky's Taboos*. Dresden, Germany: Dresden University Press, 1998.

Men' shikov, M. O. "Oskorblennyi genii." In his *Kriticheskie ocherki*, vol. 1, 262–293. St. Petersburg: Tipografiia M. Merkusheva, 1899.

Mochulsky, Konstantin. *Dostoevsky: His Life and Work*. Princeton, New Jersey: Princeton University Press, 1967.

Moore, Gene M. "The Voice of Legion: The Narrator of *The Possessed*." In *Dostoevsky Studies* 5 (1985): 51–65.

Murav, Harriet. *Holy Foolishness. Dostoevsky's Novels and the Poetics of Cultural Critique.* Stanford, CA: Stanford University Press, 1992.

Nepomnyashchy, Catherine Theimer, and Ludmilla A. Trigos. "Was Pushkin Black and Doet It Matter?" In *Under the Sky of My Africa*, edited by Catherine Theimer Nepomnyashchy, Nicole Svobodny, and Ludmilla A. Trigos. Evanston, Illinois: Northwestern University Press, 2006.

Nussbaum, Martha. *Cultivating Humanity: A Classical Defense of Reform in Liberal Education.* Cambridge, Massachusetts: Harvard University Press, 1997.

Oliva, L. Jay. *Russia in the Era of Peter the Great.* Englewood Cliffs, New Jersey: Prentice Hall, Inc., 1969.

Piksanov, N. K. "Sotsiologiia 'Goria ot uma'." In *Vek nyneshnii i vek minuvshii...*, 262–297. St. Petersburg: Azbuka-klassika, 2002.

Polevoi, A. S. "'Gore ot uma'. Komediia v chetyrekh deistviiakh, sochinenie A. S. Griboedova." *Moskovskii Telegraf* 53, no. 18 (1833).

Proskurina, Vera. *Techenie Gol' fstrima: Mikhail Gershenzon. Ego zhizn' i mif.* St. Petersburg: Aleteia, 1998.

Propp, V. Y. *Istoricheskie korni volshebnoi skazki.* Leningrad: Izdatel' stvo Leningradskogo universiteta, 1986.

Radomskaia, T. I. *Gore ot uma: "Strannaia" komediia "strannogo" sochinitelia.* Moscow: Institut mirovoi literatury imeni A. M. Gor'kogo, 2004.

Raeff, Marc. *Origins of the Russian Intelligentsia.* New York: Harcourt, Brace & World, Inc. 1966.

Ries, Nancy. *Russian Talk: Culture & Conversation during Perestroika.* Ithaca, New York: Cornell University Press, 1997.

Seckler, Dawn. "The Absence of Historical Time in Dostoevsky's *Besy*." *Studies in Slavic Cultures* 4 (2003): 57–67.

Slezkine, Yuri. *The Jewish Century.* Princeton, New Jersey: Princeton University Press, 2004.

Specter, Michael. "The Devastation." *New Yorker*, October 3, 2004.

Stepanov, Iu. S. *Konstanty: Slovar' russkoi kul'tury—opyt issledovaniia.* Moscow: Iazyki russkoi kul'tury, 1997.

Studia Russica Helsingiensia et Tartutensia 4 (1995): *"Svoe" i "chuzhoe" v literature i kul'ture.*

Terras, Victor. *Reading Dostoevsky.* Madison, Wisconsin: The University of Wisconsin Press, 1998.

Todd, William III. *The Familiar Letter as a Literary Genre in the Age of Pushkin.* Princeton, New Jersey: Princeton University Press, 1976.

———. *Fiction and Society in the Age of Pushkin.* Cambridge, Massachusetts: Harvard University Press, 1986.

Trubachev, O. N. *Istoriia slavianskikh terminov rodstva.* Moscow: Akademiia Nauk, 1959.

Vinogradov, V. V. *Istoriia slov.* Moscow: Tolk, 1994.

Wiedle, Wladimir. *Russia: Absent and Present.* New York: The John Day Company, 1952.

Yokoyama, Olga. "Russian Genderlects and Referential Expressions." *Language in Society* 28 (1999): 401–429.

———. "Speaker Imposition and Short Interlocutor Distance in Colloquial Russian." *Revue des Etudes Slaves* 66 (1995): 681–697.

———. "Oppozitsiia 'svoj-chuzhoj' v russkom iazyke." In *American Contributions to the XI International Congress of Slavists,* edited by R. A. Maguire and A. Timberlake, 452–459. Columbus, Ohio: Slavica, 1993.

Zhigulev, A, comp. *Russkie narodnye poslovitsy i pogovorki.* Moscow: Moskovskii rabochii, 1958.

Index

A
Akhmatova, Anna, 34
Aleksander I, 45, 50
Allain, Louis, 95-96
Anna Ioannovna, 40
Armenia, 87
Aronson, M., 78
Ashukin, N. S., 33
Astrakhan, 23

B
Bakhtin, N. I., 73
Begichev, S. N., 72, 75-77, 84, 86
Belinsky, Vissarion, 30, 56, 72, 101
Bem, Alfred, 94, 96
Berreby, David, 2
Beslan, 133
Bestuzhev, A. A., 33, 85-86
Bishkek, 135
Blok, Alexandr, 33, 56
Bodrov Jr., Sergei, 137n56
Bulgakov, Mikhail, 34
Bulgarin, F. V., 37, 44, 81, 85

C
Catherine the Great, 40, 46
Chavchavadze, Nino, 75
Chechnya, 134
Chekhov, Anton, 33
Chernyshevsky, Nikolai, 30
Constantinople, 27
Costello, D. P., 45, 48n23, 50, 58

D
Dagestan, 134
Dal', Vladimir, 15, 82
Derzhavin, Gavril, 73
Diogenes, 1
Dobrolyubov, Nikolai, 30
Dolgorukov, Mikhail, 22
Dolinin, A. S., 99
Don, 23
Dostoevskaya, Anna, 93
Dostoevsky, Fyodor, 7, 33, 71, 88-89, 91-122, 124-26, 129-131

Adolescent, The, 93
Brothers Karamazov, The, 93
Demons, 7, 10-11, 71, 88-89, 91, 93-101, 103-4, 106-7, 110-11, 113, 120n47, 125-26, 131
Diary of a Writer, 93
Gambler, The, 98
Idiot, The, 93, 96, 98
Insulted and the Injured, The, 92-93
Driver, Sam, 27-28, 30
Durnovo, M. S., 73

E
Ermolov, Aleksei, 41
Europe, 1, 27, 91, 123

F
Figes, Orlando, 72, 129n53
Filippov, V., 48n23
Fomichev, S. A, 50, 80, 82
Fonvizin, Denis, 30
France, 19-20, 30
Franz II, 50

G
Georgia, 40, 87, 133, 136
Gershenzon, Mikhail, 24-26, 83
Gibian, George, 71
Gnedich, N. I., 80
Gogol, Nikolai, 33, 88, 96
  Dead Souls, 88
Golburt, Luba, 54
Granovetter, Mark, 6
Grech, N. I., 44
Griboedov, Aleksandr, 6-7, 24, 31, 33-45, 47, 54, 56-58, 60, 69-78, 80-88, 91, 95-96, 100, 104, 106, 113-14, 128n52
  All in the Family, or The Married Fiancée, 41, 43-44, 63, 84
  Dmitrii Dryanskoi, 41
  Woe from Wit, 6-7, 31, 33-37, 40-42, 44-47, 53-54, 56, 60, 65-67, 69-73, 74, 76-77, 80-86, 89, 91-97, 100, 102-8, 113, 118, 122
Griboedova, Natalya, 37, 73

H
Herzen, A. I., 39-40, 117
Hobson, Mary, 45, 55n25, 64

I
Israel, 136
Istanbul, 27
Ivanov, V. V., 8-9, 11, 23, 123, 129

J
Janecek, Gerald, 61-62, 64
Jay Oliva, L., 22

K
Karamzin, N. M., 35, 97
Karatygin, P. A., 80, 84
Karlinsky, Simon, 34-35, 43-45, 61, 67
Katenin, P. A., 57, 73
Kelly, Laurence, 44-45, 65, 72, 77
Khmelnitsky, N. I., 41, 44, 84
Khvoshchinskaya, Nadezhda, 5n4
Kol'tsov, A. V., 70, 79
Koroleva, Nina, 91-92, 95, 126n51
Krylov, I. A., 33, 44, 82

L
Lebedev, A., 33, 39, 50-53, 55-56, 64
Lermontov, Mikhail, 37-38, 45, 88
    A Hero of Our Time, 88
    Death of a Poet, 37
Leskov, Nikolai, 59, 111
Lomonosov, Mikhail, 35
Lotman, Yuri, 9-10, 88, 124-26
Lubensky, Sophia, 15-16

M
Mamontov, Arkady, 133-137
Martinsen, Deborah, 97
Meerson, Olga, 110-11
Men'shikov, M. O., 51
Mochulsky, Konstantin, 96, 119-20, 126
Moore, Gene, 107n43, 120n47
Moscow, 17, 19-26, 28-31, 34, 36-37, 39-43, 46-49, 51, 53-55, 59-66, 70-80, 83, 100n37, 101-3, 118, 133
Murav, Harriet, 110-11

N
Neva, 22
Nicholas I, 45
North America, 1
Nussbaum, Martha, 1, 4

O
Ozerov, V., 41

P
Paskevich, I. F., 75
Pasternak, Boris, 5n4, 33
Paul, 29
Peter III, 39
Peter the Great, 21-22, 27, 29-30, 39, 43, 89
Piksanov, N. K., 36-38, 40, 45, 66, 69, 70, 74, 76
Pogodin, M. P., 70
Prague, 50
Propp, Vladimir, 8
Proskurina, Vera, 25n11
Pushchin, I. I., 28
Pushkin, Aleksandr, 27-31, 33-34, 37-39, 45-47, 50-51, 54, 61-63, 65-66, 70, 82, 87-88, 95-97
    A Journey from Moscow to Petersburg, 28, 30, 47
    Eugene Onegin, 66, 87-88
    Journey to Arzrum, 87
Putin, Vladimir, 133, 137

R
Radishchev, Aleksandr, 28
    A Journey from Petersburg to Moscow, 28
Radomskaya, T. I., 46-47, 50, 52-53, 56
Ries, Nancy, 5, 11, 70
Rimsky-Korsakov, Sergei, 83
Rimskaya-Korsakova, Marya Ivanovna, 24, 25n11, 83
Rogatkin, Aleksandr, 133-34
Rozanov, Vasily, 98
Ruhl, Christof, 5

S
Saltykov-Shchedrin, Mikhail, 16
    Golovlev Family, The, 16
Scott, Ridley, 11
Shakhovskoi, A. A., 41-44
Shimanovski, N. V., 71
Shishkov, A. S., 35
Shor-Chudnovskaya, Anna, 3, 131
Slezkine, Yuri, 40
Smirnov, D. A., 81-82
Smirnov, D. S., 73
Soviet Union, 12, 34, 136
Stepanov, Yuri, 11, 129n53
St. Petersburg, 22-23, 26, 29-30, 34, 40-44, 46, 51, 59, 62, 70-72, 74-78, 100n37, 103-4, 108, 115, 131
Suslova, Apollinaria Prokofievna (Polina), 98-99

T
Terras, Victor, 93, 102n42, 104

Theimer Nepomnyashchy, Catherine, 27
Tiflis (Tbilisi), 40
Todd III, William Mills, 35n14, 79-80, 88, 120n48
Tolstoy, Lev, 7, 97
   Anna Karenina, 7, 111
Tolstoy, Petr, 22
Toporov, V. N., 8-9, 11, 23, 123, 129
Trigos, Ludmilla A., 27
Trubachev, O. N., 17
Tsvetaeva, Marina, 33
Turgenev, Ivan, 34, 36
   The Diary of a Superfluous Man, 36
Turkey, 136
Tuwim, Julian, 34
Tver, 100n37
Tvertsa, 100n37

U
Ukraine, 136
United States, 136
Uralova, Valentina, 132

Uspensky, Boris, 9-10, 124-26
USSR, 134

V
Vinogradov, V. V., 60
Volga, 23, 100n37
Volkov, Solomon, 97
Vyazemsky, P. A., 37-38, 42, 44-45

W
Wasiolek, Edward, 91, 98-99, 106
Weidle, Wladimir, 19-20, 26

Y
Yankova, E. P., 6, 17-28, 36n18, 37, 42, 46, 49, 51, 74, 116, 119
   Grandmother's Stories: Memories of Five Generations, 6, 17, 23
Yokoyama, Olga, 2-3, 19

Z
Zhandr, A. A., 44, 72, 81-82
Zhigulyev, A., 15-16

www.ingramcontent.com/pod-product-compliance
Lightning Source LLC
Chambersburg PA
CBHW050527170426
43201CB00013B/2117